A WORSHIP READER

A WORSHIP READER

Short Studies and Reflections on Biblical Worship

RON MAN

Foreword by Frank Fortunato

RESOURCE *Publications* • Eugene, Oregon

A WORSHIP READER
Short Studies and Reflections on Biblical Worship

Copyright © 2025 Ron Man. All rights reserved. Except for brief quotations in critical publications or reviews, no part of this book may be reproduced in any manner without prior written permission from the publisher. Write: Permissions, Wipf and Stock Publishers, 199 W. 8th Ave., Suite 3, Eugene, OR 97401.

Resource Publications
An Imprint of Wipf and Stock Publishers
199 W. 8th Ave., Suite 3
Eugene, OR 97401

www.wipfandstock.com

PAPERBACK ISBN: 979-8-3852-5394-4
HARDCOVER ISBN: 979-8-3852-5395-1
EBOOK ISBN: 979-8-3852-5396-8

09/29/25

Artwork by Kirsten Malcolm Berry is used by permission. www.kirstenmalcolmberry.com.

Unless otherwise noted, Scripture quotations are from the ESV® Bible (The Holy Bible, English Standard Version®), copyright © 2001 by Crossway Bibles, a publishing ministry of Good News Publishers. Used by permission. All rights reserved.

In him all things hold together.
(Colossians 1:17)

Contents

Foreword by Frank Fortunato   xi

Preface   xiii

PART 1. BIBLICAL PRINCIPLES OF WORSHIP

1. Biblical Principles of Worship: Summary   3
2. Twelve Biblical Principles of Worship and Their Application to Local Church Ministry   6

PART 2. BIBLICAL AND THEOLOGICAL STUDIES

1. Revelation and Response: The Dialogue of Worship   15
2. The Gospel: A Call to Worship   19
3. "Praise and Worship": A Confusion of Terms   23

PART 3. OLD TESTAMENT STUDIES

1. The Worship Trajectory and Goal of the Entire Bible: Part 1: Old Testament   31
2. Important Themes in Old Testament Worship   36
3. The Supremacy of God's Name in the Old Testament   39
4. The Psalms: Israel's Hymnbook . . . and Ours   44
5. Is "God Inhabits the Praises of His People" Really Biblical? by Zac Hicks   51

PART 4. NEW TESTAMENT STUDIES

1. The Worship Trajectory and Goal of the Entire Bible: Part 2: New Testament — 57
2. Important Themes in New Testament Worship — 61
3. "Not Far From The Kingdom": Seeing Things God's Way (Mark 12:28–34) — 65
4. Worship and the Fall in Romans 1 — 68
5. "To him be the glory forever": Paul's Doxology in Romans 11:33–36 — 71
6. Yes and Amen: God's Program in Two Words (2 Corinthians 1:20) — 75
7. Worship in the Book of Hebrews — 79

PART 5. JESUS AND OUR WORSHIP

1. Jesus on Worship (John 4) — 89
2. Jesus, Our True Worship Leader: "What God requires, he provides." — 93
3. Towards a Christology of Worship — 107
4. Worship Leader? In Search of a Better Title — 110

PART 6. SHAPING CORPORATE WORSHIP

1. Making Our Worship More Trinitarian — 115
2. Worship and the Word — 121
3. The Call to Worship: Giving God the First Word — 127
4. Thematic Worship: A Rich Feast for the People of God — 129
5. "In Remembrance of Me" — 134

PART 7. CHURCH DYNAMICS

1. The Importance of Worship in the Church — 141
2. Managing Worship Change — 145
3. The Pastor and Worship — 149

CONTENTS

PART 8. WORSHIP AND CULTURE

1	A Letter from Tapescrew (with apologies to C. S. Lewis)	155
2	Another Letter from Tapescrew	157
3	The Bridge: Worship and Culture	159

PART 9. THE CHURCH YEAR

GOOD FRIDAY

1	The Power of the Cross: Testimonies from Church History	165

EASTER

2	Easter Sunday and Every Sunday	171
3	A Resurrection Concordance	175
4	The Glory of Easter: Others' Reflections	176
5	The Road to Understanding: An Easter Meditation (Luke 24:13–35)	180

ASCENSION

6	The Neglected Ascension	185
7	An Ascension Concordance	188
8	A Service of Worship for Ascension Sunday (Second Presbyterian Church, Memphis, Tennessee, May 28, 1995)	190
9	A Responsive Reading for Ascension Sunday (First Evangelical Church, Memphis, Tennessee, May 28, 1995)	194

PENTECOST

10	The Holy Spirit and Worship	196
11	The Spirit's Coming: Some Rich Quotes	202

REFORMATION SUNDAY

12	The Reformation of Worship	206
13	Celebrating the "Solas" of the Reformation in Worship	210

CONTENTS

CHRISTMAS

14 Worship the King: A Second Look at Matthew 2 — 214
15 A Christmas Festival of Lessons and Carols — 218

Bibliography — 227
Index — 233

Foreword

As an enthusiastic consumer of Ron Man's monthly online *Worship Notes* (worship-resources.org/content-type/worship-notes), I am delighted that he has now distilled more than two decades of those writings into a usable, thematic compendium. Dr. Man has provided Christian worship leaders and theologians with an invaluable, accessible guidebook on understanding, planning, and leading worship, supplementing his earlier volumes: *Proclamation and Praise: Hebrews 2:12 and the Christology of Worship*; the massive *Let Us Draw Near: Biblical Foundations of Worship*; and the condensed version of the latter volume, *The New and Living Way: Invitation to Biblical Worship*; as well as the many other resources available at worship-resources.org. All of Man's writings, including *A Worship Reader*, show a commitment to John Stott's insistence that "there can be *no theology without doxology*," and "*no doxology without theology.*"

One of the most helpful contributions of the volume is Man's *Biblical Principles of Worship*. He has condensed the sixty-page discussion of twelve concluding principles from *Let Us Draw Near* into a "Reader's Digest" version that also includes practical, concise applications for church settings.

There are many nuances of biblical, theological, cultural, and missional aspects of worship addressed in this present volume. Some of the areas covered include: the foundational "Revelation and Response" pattern of worship; some key Old and New Testament passages and principles; the critical understanding of Jesus Christ as the true Leader of our worship; deep dives into the richness of Romans and Hebrews; practical issues relating to corporate worship in the church; studies relating to key events in the church year; and Man's helpful Bridge illustration, which addresses the interplay of Scripture and culture.

FOREWORD

Man also confronts and challenges some "sacred cows" along the way: what the "praise and worship" nomenclature in fact implies; did the Magi actually "worship" the baby Jesus?; and does God really "inhabit the praises of his people"? (drawing on the work of Zac Hicks for the latter discussion). And Man's "Tapescrew Letters" (a take-off on C. S. Lewis' *Screwtape Letters*) offer clever and convicting insights into our worship motives and foibles. In many ways the volume could serve as a medicine chest to treat common worship ailments.

I first heard some of the insights found in the *Reader* at a global gathering in 2006 where Man spoke and also quoted James Torrance, one of his favorite theologians:

> Whenever true worship happens, it is because Jesus Christ is in the midst of his people, leading them in their praises and presenting them to the Father as part of his own perfect offering of praise. James Torrance says that "worship is the gift of participating through the Spirit in the incarnate Son's communion with the Father" [*Worship, Community and the Triune God of Grace*, 30].

Hearing that quote for the first time overwhelmed me. While serving as the emcee at that global gathering, I had to follow Dr. Man's homily and had to give the trivial announcements. However, I remained transfixed as I tried to grasp the implications of the quotation, namely the intimacy among the Trinity. I stepped onto the podium and could not find my voice. Speechless and mesmerized, it took several moments for my brain to refocus and to concentrate on giving the announcements. Reading the Torrance quote again in the *Reader*, I experienced a *déjà vu* moment being reminded of this riveting truth.

Worship leaders and worshipers will continue to use Ron Man's teachings and resources throughout the world in any worship setting. I will be ever grateful for the privilege of interacting with Ron Man, both as a friend and through his powerful writings that include *A Worship Reader*.

FRANK FORTUNATO
International Worship Mentor
Operation Mobilization

Preface

These short studies are compiled from issues of *Worship Notes*, the author's monthly online newsletter, which has now been running for twenty years (all issues can be accessed at worship-resources.org/content-type/worship-notes/). The collection here is arranged thematically and covers a wide range of biblical, theological, and practical topics of interest to pastors, worship pastors, worship leaders, and thoughtful laypeople. And the compact nature of each study provides a manageable and accessible vehicle for study and reflection.

Many thanks to my friend James Brown, Director of Music for many years at Independent Presbyterian Church in Memphis, Tennessee, who first suggested to me that I write such a newsletter to provide succinct, bite-sized readings for busy church musicians and others.

PART 1

Biblical Principles of Worship

1

Biblical Principles of Worship
Summary

1. DOXOLOGICAL WORSHIP: God's glory, and our joyful celebration of it in worship, should be the focus and goal of all life and ministry.

   For from him and through him and to him are all things. To him be glory forever. Amen.
   (Romans 11:36)

2. THEOCENTRIC WORSHIP: Worship is first and foremost for God.

   "Worship God."
   (Revelation 19:10; 22:9)

3. DIALOGICAL WORSHIP: Worship is a dialogue between God and His people, a rhythm of revelation and response.

   For all the promises of God find their Yes in him [Christ]. That is why it is through him that we utter our Amen to God for his glory.
   (2 Corinthians 1:20)

4. WORD-SATURATED WORSHIP: The Word must be central in our worship.

   Let the word of Christ dwell in you richly, teaching and admonishing one another in all wisdom, singing psalms and hymns and spiritual songs, with thankfulness in your hearts to God.
   (Colossians 3:16)

PART 1. BIBLICAL PRINCIPLES OF WORSHIP

5. PARTICIPATORY WORSHIP: Worship is the responsibility of all of God's people.

   Oh, magnify the LORD with me,
   and let us exalt his name together! (Psalm 34:3)

6. CHRIST-LED WORSHIP: Our worship is acceptable in and through Christ our High Priest.

   Through him [Christ] then let us continually offer up a sacrifice of
   praise to God, that is, the fruit of lips that acknowledge his name.
   (Hebrews 13:15)

7. SPIRIT-ENABLED WORSHIP: Our response of worship is enabled, motivated and empowered by the Holy Spirit.

   We are the true circumcision, who worship by the Spirit of God and
   glory in Christ Jesus and put no confidence in the flesh.
   (Philippians 3:3)

8. WHOLE-LIFE WORSHIP: Worship is the response of our entire lives to God.

   I appeal to you therefore, brethren, by the mercies of God, to pres-
   ent your bodies as a living sacrifice, holy and acceptable to God,
   which is your spiritual worship.
   (Romans 12:1)

9. HEART WORSHIP: God is much more concerned with our *heart* than with the *form* of our worship.

   "Man looks on the outward appearance, but the LORD looks on the
   heart."
   (1 Samuel 16:7)

10. EDIFYING WORSHIP: Worship should promote the unity and edification of the body.

    May the God of endurance and encouragement grant you to live in
    such harmony with one another, in accord with Christ Jesus, that
    together you may with one voice glorify the God and Father of our
    Lord Jesus Christ.
    (Romans 15:5–6)

11. TRANS-GENERATIONAL WORSHIP: Young and old need each other in the body of Christ.

> *Young men and maidens together, old men and children! Let them praise the name of the LORD, for his name alone is exalted.*
> *(Psalm 148:12–13; cf. Titus 2:2–8)*

12. TAUGHT WORSHIP: These things must be taught and re-taught.

> *Finally then, brethren, we ask and urge you in the Lord Jesus, that as you received from us how you ought to walk and to please God, just as you are doing, that you do so more and more.*
> *(1 Thessalonians 4:1)*

2

Twelve Biblical Principles of Worship
and Their Application to Local Church Ministry

INTRODUCTION

The good news about worship in our day is that it is a subject which, after many years of general neglect (A. W. Tozer called worship "The Missing Jewel of the Evangelical Church"), is receiving well-deserved attention and emphasis. The bad news is that worship has become an issue about which there is much conflict and divisiveness in our churches.

The following document is an attempt to crystallize some guiding principles of worship from Scripture (in the absence of detailed prescriptions for worship in the pages of the New Testament). Each principle is stated, scripturally supported, and briefly expounded; then in each case there is a "Therefore" paragraph describing how this principle could be fleshed out in the worship life of a local congregation.

Corporate worship involves attitudes and acts of praise and adoration in response to God for his greatness, goodness, and grace—including praying, preaching singing, giving, etc.— at the invitation of and under the authority of the Word of God. We want to stand firmly on biblical ground in the ordering of worship in our churches, while allowing for the variety and freedom which the New Testament allows and avoiding "teaching as doctrine the precepts of men." Above all we want to glorify in our worship the One who is deserving of all praise.

DOXOLOGICAL WORSHIP: God's glory, and our joyful celebration of it in worship, should be the focus and goal of all life and ministry.

For from him and through him and to him are all things. To him be glory forever. Amen. (Rom 11:36)

Worship is an end it itself. By definition other types of ministry necessarily have horizontal, people-focused aspects; but worship is purely vertically focused. It is the primary purpose for which God created us, and therefore our highest endeavor and greatest fulfillment (Isa 43:6–7; Ps 16:11; Matt 22:35–38; 1 Pet 4:11).

THEREFORE: We shall give worship careful focus and attention in the life of this church. We will relate all of our activities to it and to the goal of magnifying the glory of God. We will make explicit God's glory as our most important pursuit, aim, and preoccupation.

THEOCENTRIC WORSHIP: Worship is first and foremost for God.

"Worship God." (Rev 19:10; 22:9)

God is the subject and object of worship; it is about him and for him. As God, he is absolutely unique and therefore the only One worthy of our praise; as Creator, he and he alone is deserving of the worship of his creatures and of his creation (Rom 11:36; Ps 148:1–13).

THEREFORE: We will focus on glorifying the Lord in our worship, and on offering up a suitable and appropriate sacrifice of praise to his name. Our supreme motivation in our worship will be his pleasure rather than our own fulfillment or enjoyment. We will come to give more than to receive, yet realizing that we only have something to give because of God's prior gracious giving to us.

PART 1. BIBLICAL PRINCIPLES OF WORSHIP

> **DIALOGICAL WORSHIP:** Worship is a dialogue between God and his people, a rhythm of revelation and response.

For all the promises of God find their Yes in him [Christ]. That is why it is through him that we utter our Amen to God for his glory.
(2 Cor 1:20)

In worship God speaks to us through his Word; and we respond with our hearts, voices, and bodies. The impartation of *theology* is not complete until it is answered with appropriate *doxology*. This pattern is seen throughout Scripture: God always acts first to reveal himself and to reach out to human beings; all worship is a response to God's prior revealing and saving initiative (Ps 48:10; 150:2; 2 Cor. 1:20).

THEREFORE: We will allow for a healthy balance of the Word proclaimed (through preaching, Scripture readings and Scripture-based songs) and the people's response (in song, prayer, confession, testimony and the Lord's Supper). We will allow adequate time for response after the sermon. We will also celebrate the Lord's Supper regularly; and will give it its proper due, as a primary response to God's grace, by allowing sufficient time for it.

> **WORD-SATURATED WORSHIP:** The Word must be central in our worship.

Let the word of Christ dwell in you richly, teaching and admonishing one another in all wisdom, singing psalms and hymns and spiritual songs, with thankfulness in your hearts to God. (Col 3:16)

Worship is our creaturely response to God's self-revelation. We are responsible to praise him as he really is, not as we would suppose or hope him to be. God has revealed himself and his glory through the inspired Scriptures. (Ps 56:4; 138:2)

THEREFORE: We will read the Word, pray the Word, preach the Word, and sing the Word in our corporate and private worship. We will allow the Word to invite us to worship, to provide the context and motivation for our worship, to inform and enrich and fuel our worship. We will avoid just singing human thoughts about God instead of what he has told us about himself in Scripture.

PARTICIPATORY WORSHIP: Worship is the responsibility of all of God's people.

Oh, magnify the LORD with me, and let us exalt his name together!
(Ps 34:3)

Worship is a verb; it is something we do, not something we watch. An important expression of the priesthood of all believers is that every individual has a vital role to play in the corporate worship of the church (Ps 107:32; Rom 15:5–6).

THEREFORE: We will further whole-hearted participation in worship in every way possible: by encouraging week-long worship and spiritual preparation for corporate worship, by enhancing the physical environment for worship (and not overwhelming the voices of the congregation with an overly loud sound system), by carefully selecting the music for worship (using substantial, singable, mostly familiar songs), and by giving opportunity for corporate prayer and Scripture reading.

CHRIST-LED WORSHIP: Our worship is acceptable in and through Christ our High Priest.

Through him [Christ] then let us continually offer up a sacrifice of praise to God, that is, the fruit of lips that acknowledge his name.
(Heb 13:15)

Jesus Christ is the Leader of our worship. We come in him and by his worthiness into God's presence, and he gathers up our modest worship into his own perfect offering. (Heb 8:1–2; 10:19–22)

THEREFORE: We will strive for excellence in our worship, but not see technical expertise or artistic merit as ends in themselves, or as a means to gain God's favor or acceptance. We will encourage a mindset of service rather than performance among our worship leaders, realizing that ultimately our worship is pleasing to God only because we come through Christ.

PART 1. BIBLICAL PRINCIPLES OF WORSHIP

> **SPIRIT-ENABLED WORSHIP: Our response of worship is enabled, motivated and empowered by the Holy Spirit.**

We are the true circumcision, who worship by the Spirit of God and glory in Christ Jesus and put no confidence in the flesh.
(Phil 3:3)

As God, the Holy Spirit deserves our adoration and praise as much as the Father and the Son. Yet he chooses to glorify not himself but rather to point us to Christ (John 16:14) and thus lead us to the Father in worship. Jesus Christ is the Way into the Father's presence; the Holy Spirit is our Guide. We *can* come to the Father in worship because of the work of Christ; we *want to* come into the Father's presence in worship because of the work of the Holy Spirit, assuring us of our standing by grace (Rom 8:14–17) and filling us for the work of praise (Eph 5:18–19).

THEREFORE: We will not focus unduly on the Holy Spirit in our worship, but seek to exalt Christ (1 Cor. 12:3) as the Spirit himself desires to do. We will humbly seek the Spirit's help in our weakness to enable us to desire, pray to, and worship God (Rom 8:28). We will rest in the Spirit's divine enablement to the glory of God (Rom 8:3–4)

> **WHOLE-LIFE WORSHIP: Worship is the response of our entire lives to God.**

I appeal to you therefore, brethren, by the mercies of God, to present your bodies as a living sacrifice, holy and acceptable to God, which is your spiritual worship.
(Rom 12:1)

Worship is not just a weekly event, but rather a way of living in dependence upon and gratitude towards our gracious Lord. While corporate worship is an important expression of that walk of worship, it must be fueled by lives of personal and private devotion and faithfulness (John 4:21–24; 1 Cor 10:31). Worship is also the expression of the totality of our being—mind, emotions, will, actions: all that we are responding to all that God is (Ps 135:5; 100:3–4; 22:22; 98:4; Heb 13:15–16).

THEREFORE: We will teach the importance of and promote a lifestyle of worship. We will magnify the glory of God as the focus and goal of all of life. We will treat corporate worship not as an interruption of everyday life, but rather as a gathered celebration of the God who makes life worth living.

HEART WORSHIP: God is much more concerned with our heart than with the form of our worship.

> "Man looks on the outward appearance, but the Lord looks on the heart."
> (1 Sam 16:7)

The New Testament (in contrast to the Old Testament) is remarkably non-prescriptive when it comes to the shape and form of corporate worship services; we can only assume that God intended to allow considerable freedom in these areas. Both Testaments, on the other hand, are very clear about how seriously God takes the heart attitude and motivation of one's worship (2 Chr 30:18–20; Mark 12:33).

THEREFORE: We will stress the inward reality of worship and remain flexible in our approach to form.

EDIFYING WORSHIP: Worship should promote the unity and edification of the body.

> May the God of endurance and encouragement grant you to be in such harmony with one another, in accord with Christ Jesus, that together you may with one voice glorify the God and Father of our Lord Jesus Christ.
> (Rom 15:5–6)

The body of Christ is not an affinity group, but rather a disparate band of saved sinners that only the Spirit can unify. We must fight the rampant individualism of our age and of our natures, and actively encourage the building up of the body (Eph 4:1–6, 15–16; 5:19–21; Col 3:12–17; Heb 10:23–25).

THEREFORE: We will exult in our diversity and seek to learn from one another various expressions of worship (Eph 5:19; Col 3:16). We will avoid novelty for its own sake, however, and will always strive to keep the health of the whole body in mind when it comes to innovation or change in worship. We will not seek to promote our personal agendas or preferences in worship, but rather prayerfully and deliberately seek the good of

PART 1. BIBLICAL PRINCIPLES OF WORSHIP

the body as a whole. We will exhort one another to consider another's needs before our own (Rom 12:10; Phil 2:2–3), and to look beyond self to our corporate identity in Christ.

TRANS-GENERATIONAL WORSHIP: Young and old need each other in the body of Christ.

> *Young men and maidens together, old men and children!*
> *Let them praise the name of the LORD, for his name alone is exalted.*
> *(Ps 148:12–13; cf. Tit 2:2–8)*

The diversity of the body of Christ necessarily and significantly includes the mixing of generations. Young people are to honor and learn from the stability and heritage of their elders, while the young can add new energy and fresh expressions of worship (Ps 79:13; 149:1; Titus 2:2–8).

THEREFORE: We will respect the special contributions of young and old, and seek to involve and engage all groups in our services without giving preference to one over another. We will seek to use godly discernment in evaluating all materials used in our corporate worship.

TAUGHT WORSHIP: These things must be taught and re-taught.

> *Finally then, brethren, we ask and urge you in the Lord Jesus, that*
> *as you received from us how you ought to walk and to please God,*
> *just as you are doing, that you do so more and more.*
> *(1 Thess 4:1)*

The above truths are important elements of Christian understanding and discipleship, but must be consistently and persistently taught if they are to lodge in hearts and change attitudes and behaviors (2 Pet 1:12–13). Otherwise we all tend to revert to a default mode that has ourselves at the center.

THEREFORE: We will teach these principles and exhort one another to grow in these areas. We will seek to model these truths before one another in our congregation, and as an example to our community and to the wider body of Christ.

PART 2

Biblical and Theological Studies

1

Revelation and Response
The Dialogue of Worship

The rhythm of *Revelation and Response* is characteristic of all God's dealings with humanity. And this ordering of these two elements is tremendously significant, for it speaks of the initiative which God takes, and the lengths to which he goes, to ensure a relationship with those whom he chooses. Throughout Scripture we see God's revelatory initiative with his people, with the result that all worship, obedience, and service should be seen as a response to God's prior activity in revelation and redemption. This is true because, as Eric Alexander has stated, "God needs to be known before he can be worshiped."[1] Nicholls expands on this idea: "Our worship is our answer to God who has first addressed us. Man worships the God who has made himself known. We 'praise his holy Name'—that is, we worship him in his self-revelation."[2]

Calvin speaks also to this natural progression: "The proclamation of God's praises is always promoted by the teaching of the gospel; for as soon as God becomes known to us, His infinite praises resound in our hearts and ears."[3] To which Butin adds:

1. Alexander, "Worship: The Old Testament Pattern."
2. Nicholls, *Jacob's Ladder: The Meaning of Worship*, 37.
3. Calvin, *Commentaries on the Epistle to the Hebrews*, on 2:12.

> The initiatory "downward" movement of Christian worship begins in the Father's gracious and free revelation of the divine nature to the church through the Son, by means of the Spirit. In more concrete terms, this takes place in the proclamation of the Word according to Scripture, by the empowerment and illumination of the Spirit. . . . The "upward" movement of human response in worship—focused around prayer and the celebration of the sacraments—is also fundamentally motivated by God. Human response—"the sacrifice of praise and thanksgiving"—arises from the faith that has its source in the indwelling Holy Spirit. In that Spirit, prayer, devotion, and obedience are offered to God the Father . . . through the Son Jesus Christ.[4]

Worship is a *dialogue* between God and his people: that means that our services should alternate and balance elements of revelation and response: hearing from God (through his Word, read and sung and prayed and preached) and replying to him (with our songs, prayers, confessions, and the Lord's Supper). Historically, this pattern underlies both Old Testament worship (in covenant establishment and renewal) and Christian worship (in the Word-Table structure found in most historical liturgies).

But revelation should *precede* response: we should let God have the first word, and be careful to *listen* before we *speak*. Too many services launch right into singing; but that means we are responding before we have heard anything to respond to! This does violence to the biblical pattern, and to God's preeminence. Until we have heard from God, we have nothing to say to him—we must worship him as he really is, not as we (or the songwriters) imagine or hope him to be. In this light, a "Call to Worship" is anything but outdated. Indeed, whether read or sung or prayed, it is an acknowledgement that we have come to worship God at his invitation and by and through his Word.

Martin Luther understood this principle. On the glass door leading to the sanctuary of the Castle Church in Wittenberg, Germany (the church where he posted his 95 Theses), there is engraved a quotation from the great Reformer:

> It should always happen in this house of God that the Lord *speaks to us* through his holy word, and that we then *speak to him* with our prayers and songs of praise.

---

4. Butin, *Revelation, Redemption, and Response*, 102.

BIBLICAL EXAMPLES

The pattern of revelation resulting in response, of theology leading to doxology, of God's action causing human reaction, is a common biblical paradigm:

	REVELATION	RESPONSE
Life of Abraham	Covenantal promises, names of God, theophanies	Abraham builds altars, calls on the name of the Lord
Exodus	Revelation of God's nature (Exod 3; Sinai), redemption from Egypt	Song of Moses; sacrifices as the response of a redeemed people
10 Commandments	"I am the Lord your God, who brought you out of the land of Egypt" (Exod 20:2)	[Therefore] "you shall have no other gods before me" (Exod 20:3); etc.
Psalm 1:2	"The Law of the Lord . . ."	"is his delight."
Psalm 48:10	"As is your name, O God . . ."	"So is your praise to the end of the earth."
Psalm 96:4	"Great is the LORD . . ."	"And greatly to be praised."
Psalm 100	"The LORD is God" 3 "The LORD is good" 5	"shout/serve/come" 1–2 "enter/praise/give thanks" 4
Psalm 150:2	. . . "according to his excellent greatness."	"Praise him . . ."
Isaiah 6	"I saw the LORD" 2–4	"Woe is me!" 5
	pardon, call to service 6–8a	"Send me!" 8b
Luke 1–2	Annunciation to Mary & visit to Elizabeth 1:26–45	MAGNIIFICAT 1:46–55
	Annunciation to Zacharias & birth of John 1:5–25; 57–66	BENEDICTUS 1:67–79
	Angel's announcement 2:8–12	GLORIA 2:13–14
	Simeon sees the Christ 2:25–27	NUNC DIMITTIS 2:28–32
Romans 1:20–21	God's attributes, power, nature "clearly seen"; "they knew God"	but "they did not honor him as God or give thanks"
2 Corinthians 1:20	God says "Yes" to us in Christ	We reply "Amen" through Christ
Hebrews 2:12	"I will proclaim your name to my brethren"	"and in the midst of the congregation I will sing your praise"
Hebrews 3:1	Jesus as "Apostle"	Jesus as "High Priest"

PART 2. BIBLICAL AND THEOLOGICAL STUDIES

QUOTATIONS

"All our worship is but our response to the self-giving of God in revelation and redemption." (William Nicholls, *Jacob's Ladder: The Meaning of Worship*, 53)

"Biblical faith is uncompromisingly and unembarrassedly dialogical." (Walter Brueggemann, *The Psalms and the Life of Faith*, 68)

"Worship is a conversation between the God of revelation and people in need of redemption." (C. Welton Gaddy, *The Gift of Worship*, xvii)

"The distinctive genius of corporate worship is the two-beat rhythm of revelation and response. God speaks; we answer. God acts; we accept and give. God gives; we receive." (Ralph Martin, *The Worship of God: Some Theological, Pastoral, and Practical Reflections*, 6)

"Worship is a dialogue, but the initial call comes from God who begins the conversation." (Richard Paquier, *Dynamics of Worship: Foundations and Uses of Liturgy*, 8)

"Worship depends upon revelation, and Christian worship depends upon the revelation of God in Jesus Christ. Worship, that is to say, begins not from our end but from God's; it springs from the divine initiative in redemption. We come to God because God, in Jesus Christ, has come to us: we love Him because He first loved us: we ascribe to Him supreme worth because He has showed Himself to be worthy of our complete homage, gratitude and trust. Worship is essentially a response, man's response to God's Word of grace, to what He has done for us men and for our salvation." (Raymond Abba, *Principles of Christian Worship*, 5)

[*Worship Notes* 1.5, May 2006]

2

The Gospel: A Call to Worship

THE CENTRAL ISSUE

In the fall, mankind refused to give to God the worship that he alone deserves, and which people were created to give. In Paul's words, "although they knew God, they did not honor him as God or give thanks to him" (Rom 1:21). Satan in the form of the serpent claimed in Genesis 3:5 that Eve could be "like God"—this was his lie, and the root of Lucifer's own rebellion against God, as suggested in Isaiah 14:14: "I will make myself like the Most High."

In wanting some of God's unique glory, Adam and Eve robbed him of that exclusive worship which was his due. Romans 1 makes it clear that the fall is not just a fall into immoral attitudes or behavior—those are rather consequences of the fall. The fall involves a decision about God in relationship to man: *"Whom are you going to worship?"* was the issue. And that indeed is the most important question facing every man, woman, and child in the world: "Who is going to be on the throne of your life? Who is going to be at the center of your existence? Whom are you going to worship?"

By answering that question wrongly, and denying to God his unique position as Creator, Adam and Eve inevitably turned to false worship; they "worshiped and served the creature rather than the Creator" (Rom 1:25).

PART 2. BIBLICAL AND THEOLOGICAL STUDIES

THE GREAT REVERSAL

God sent Christ to undo the effects of sin outlined in Romans 1, so that we might begin to: worship the Creator rather than the creature (cf. 1:25); exchange images and idols for "the glory of the immortal God" (1:23); and "honor him as God and give thanks to him" (1:21). As A.W. Tozer put it:

> Why did Christ come? Why was He conceived? Why was He born? Why was He crucified? Why did He rise again? Why is He now at the right hand of the Father?
>
> The answer to all these questions is, "in order that He might make worshipers out of rebels; in order that He might restore us again to the place of worship we knew when we first created."[1]

It is significant that in the very last chapter of the Bible we find a reminder of Scripture's central theme and focus (and, in the context of that chapter, the ultimate and final reversal of the fall's corrupted worship): the angel replies firmly to John's misdirected reverence (falling down to worship the angel, Rev 22:8) with the clarion call (which reverberates through all of the Bible and all of history) to "Worship *God!*" (22:9c).

THE GOSPEL CALL TO WORSHIP

If the issue in the fall was robbing God of the worship he deserves, and if the work of Christ was intended to restore that worship, then the gospel is in fact a call to lay aside false gods and idols and to worship the One who made us. Though we don't often think of the gospel in those terms, that is in fact what we see in Revelation 14:6–7. John writes:

> And I saw another angel flying in midheaven, having an eternal *gospel* to preach to those who live on the earth, and to every nation and tribe and tongue and people; and he said with a loud voice, "Fear God, and give him glory, because the hour of his judgment has come; worship him who made the heaven and the earth and sea and springs of waters."

The "eternal gospel" which the angel preaches to those on earth involves three intersecting commands or calls: to fear God, to give him glory, and to worship him. How closely these relate to what Romans 1 says we have taken from God! Indeed, David Peterson wrote, "In line with other New

---

1. Tozer, *Worship: The Missing Jewel*.

Testament passages, Revelation 14:6–7 suggests that evangelism may be viewed as a call to worship God appropriately."[2]

What we see here is a *God-centered* rather than a man-centered perspective on the gospel. Yes, God loves us, and has sent his Son to save us from our sins and make us his children. But that is a means toward an even greater end, and not the ultimate goal. As we see from the perspective that Romans 1 gives us on biblical history and its basic conflict, that ultimate goal is for God to be honored and glorified in worship as he alone deserves to be.

THE GOSPEL CALL FROM FALSE TO TRUE WORSHIP

Too often we describe the gospel only in negative terms: being saved from God's wrath, turning from sin, escaping hell; it is certainly all these things, but it also involves turning *to* something as well as *away* from something. When we receive the gospel, we turn to God, and that necessarily involves turning from false worship to true worship. This is suggested by these words of Paul:

> For they themselves report about us what kind of a reception we had with you, and how you turned to God from idols to serve a living and true God. (1 Thess 1:9)

The Thessalonians rejected their former worship of idols and gave themselves and their worship to the Creator.

Similarly, when the inhabitants of Lystra wanted to offer sacrifices to Paul and Barnabas as gods, the missionaries replied:

> "Men, why are you doing these things? We also are men, of like nature with you, and we bring you good news, that you should turn from these vain things to a living God, who made the heaven and the earth and the sea and all that is in them." (Acts 14:15)

Here we see again the themes from Romans 1—God is the Creator, the living God who alone is worthy of our worship; we are called by the "good news" (the gospel) to turn away from "these vain things" (which in the context involved the worship of idols and of false gods, including Paul and Barnabas!).

Similarly, Paul reports Jesus as saying to him at his conversion:

---

2. Peterson, *Engaging with God*, 266.

"I am sending you to open their eyes, so that they may turn from darkness to light and from the power of Satan to God." (Acts 26:18)

THE GOAL OF THE GOSPEL

The work of Christ (his past redemptive work and also his present priestly ministry) has won for us the inestimable privilege of drawing near to God (Heb 10:19–22) to enjoy his presence and to glorify him with our worship. That direct access to God is what we lost in the Garden, and which Christ came to restore through the gospel. By the power of the gospel unto salvation (Rom 1:16), we take our proper place in the created order, even as we joyfully give God the highest place, the place of all honor and glory.

Fanny Crosby understood this and expressed it in the refrain of her hymn "To God Be the Glory":

> O come to the Father
> *[the blessing of the gospel: access to the Father]*
> through Jesus the Son;
> *[the means of that access]*
> And give Him the glory,
> *[the ultimate goal of the gospel: God's glory]*
> great things He hath done.
> *[the basis for our praise]*

*See also Ron Man, "False and True Worship in Romans 1" at tinyurl.com/falseandtrue

[*Worship Notes* 2.7, July 2007]

3

"Praise and Worship"
A Confusion of Terms

JUST WHAT IS WORSHIP?

Everybody's talking about it, but are we talking about the same thing? C. E. B. Cranfield points out:

> We may distinguish three uses of the word "worship"; (i) to denote a particular element of what is generally referred to as worship, namely, adoration; (ii) to denote generally the public worship of the religious community gathered together and also the private religious exercises of the family and the individual; and (iii), in a still wider sense, to denote the whole life of the community or of the individual viewed as service of God.[1]

Many writers build their definition of worship on the derivation of the word from the Old English "worthship." But, of course, to derive a truly biblical meaning one must explore the biblical terms themselves; and a number of different scriptural words are rendered as "worship" in various English translations. For more on the nuances of these terms, see the extended treatment in David Peterson's definitive *Engaging with God: A Biblical Theology of Worship*.

---

1. C. E. B. Cranfield, "Divine and Human Action," 387.

PART 2. BIBLICAL AND THEOLOGICAL STUDIES

PRAISE AND/OR WORSHIP??

The confusion is compounded when it comes to the ubiquitous use of the phrase "Praise and Worship." This grouping of words is commonly used nowadays as a synonym for contemporary worship or contemporary worship music. For instance, Wikipedia has given this explanation:

> The phrase praise and worship is normally used within Christianity. It can refer to:
> - The overall praise and worship of God—see Christian worship
> - A style of music — see Contemporary worship music
> - A time of congregational singing—see Contemporary worship

We see many churches offering a "Praise and Worship Service" as either their regular fare or as a new, alternative service; Praise and Worship albums are released all the time; Word Music and other publishers produce collections of song/hymns/ arrangements "for Praise and Worship." In fact, the words "praise and worship" are used together with such frequency today that few are aware anymore of the origins of the construction and its original implications.

Common use of the phrase developed in the early days of the charismatic movement in the 1960s, and at that time carried with it a quite specific understanding of the worship service and its structure. Some charismatic articulators of worship theology claimed that certain Psalms suggest a structure for corporate worship that involves a movement through the service from louder, more boisterous singing (which they termed "praise") to an eventual level of quiet, meditative engagement with God characterized by slower, more reflective songs ("entering into his presence," and designated as "worship"). Advocates for this kind of progression claim support for their view in such passages as Psalms 95, 96, and 100. And so we read statements such as these:

> Praise prepares us for worship . . . The order is praise first, worship second [citing Psalm 95:1-2 and 96:4-8]. . . . Praise is often loudly exuberant while worship is more apt to be quietly exultant. . . . Praise puts love into words and action while worship puts love into touch and relationship. . . . Praise . . . is the route to worship. . . . We do not desire to remain in praise when God's presence makes worship a distinct possibility.[2]

---

2. Judson Cornwall, "Praise and Worship," 121-22.

> Praise can be conceived of as a gateway to worship.... Starting with praise will help worship flow more easily.... Praise is horizontal in its purpose, while worship is primarily a vertical interaction.... Praise can sometimes be distant, but worship is usually intimate.... Worship is different. It brings us close to the heart of God.[3]

This understanding was sometimes carried over into publications that were intended for a broader audience:

> The worship service becomes a journey into His presence. "Enter His gates with thanksgiving, and His courts with praise (Ps 100:4). Thanksgiving and praise move us into His presence. Worship occurs when we are before Him.... Songs of thanksgiving are usually fast, lively, loud and joyful... The personality of praise is one of joyful celebration, exaltation and majestic splendor.... The character of worship is one of quietness, reverence, tenderness and serenity.[4]

> The function of worship is to express love to God. The function of praise is to celebrate the works, ways and character of God.[5]

As Don Hustad points out, under this view "thanksgiving, praise, and worship are different, consecutive experiences of the community of faith."[6]

EVALUATION

1. A common pitfall in mining the Scriptures for guidelines for worship, and one that is not at all unique to the charismatic movement, is the tendency to confuse what is *descriptive* and what is intended to be *prescriptive*. In other words, just because something is done in the Bible or a particular pattern is found does not automatically mean that that act or form is intended by God to be normative for us. It may or it may not: we must carefully examine what the biblical writers (and the Holy Spirit) are intending to communicate, in the absence of an explicit command or "go and do likewise." As Timothy Quill has

---

3. Sorge, *Exploring Worship*, 69, 68.
4. Barker, *Songs for Praise and Worship*, 474.
5. McMinn, "The Praise Transition," in Fettke, *The Celebration Hymnal: Worship Resource Edition*, 16.
6. Hustad, *True Worship*, 120.

put it: "Careful exegesis must determine what is descriptive and what is prescriptive for worship today."[7]

For instance, while Isaiah 6 can indeed provide a helpful pattern for a worship service, it is going too far to assert, as some do, that the passage provides *the* biblical pattern for worship; there is simply no warrant in the text for making that claim.

The same is true when it comes to the idea of a required progression from thanksgiving to praise to worship, based on texts such as Psalm 95, 96, and 100. Observing such a pattern in the text (or finding it helpful in practice) does not mean (without further support) that it is intended to be *normative*. It may be profitably used without making it a non-negotiable for faithful or meaningful worship.

2. To define "worship" as a merely inward act simply does not do justice to the biblical usage (in the original languages or as commonly translated). There are plenty of biblical examples where "worship" involves outward acts and public displays.

3. We must deal with the biblical terms themselves and not merely with approximate English equivalents. Yet it is safe to say that the biblical concept of "worship" encompasses a broader category (including aspects of corporate and private devotion, as well as lifestyle implications), while "praise" (along with thanksgiving, confession, petition, intercession, etc.) is but one more focused subset of that broader concept of worship. Don Hustad concurs: "In historic Christian thought, worship is defined as the overall activity of believers in their . . . gatherings, and it includes every affirmative response to God: praise, thanksgiving, confession, dedication (submission), and petition."[8]

CONCLUSION

Bob Kauflin cautions:

> Perhaps we can say that, according to Scripture, "worship" is our response to God's self-revelation in ways that please him, and "praise" is an aspect of worship. But when biblical terms such as

---

7. Quill, "Response to Ligon Duncan," in Pinson, *Perspectives on Christian Worship*, 127.
8. Hustad, *True Worship*, 120.

these become a mere verbal shorthand for different musical styles, we are much the poorer for it.[9]

Undoubtedly, the phrase "Praise and Worship" is here to stay. But let's understand its limitations and use more accurate designations for contemporary worship music and contemporary services. We need to acknowledge the vast reach of the Bible's call to *worship*: "whether you eat or drink, or whatever you do, do *all* to the glory of God" (1 Cor 10:31), and worship him with our lives, our relationships, our service, our repentance, our dependence . . . and our praise.

[*Worship Notes* 3.7, July 2008]

---

9. Kauflin, *Worship Matters* blog, October 14, 2003.

PART 3

Old Testament Studies

1

The Worship Trajectory and Goal of the Entire Bible
Part 1: Old Testament

Scott W. Hahn, in his article "Canon, Cult and Covenant: The Promise of Liturgical Hermeneutics,"[1] has given a fascinating overview of the entire spectrum of biblical revelation as centered in and heading towards worship. In fact, he shows how each major movement in the scriptural record culminates in worship. The treatment below draws heavily on Hahn's insights.

> There is a liturgical reason and purpose for the creation of the world and the human person, and there is a liturgical "destiny" toward which creation and the human person journey in the pages of the canonical text. At each decisive stage in God's covenant relations with humanity, the divine-human relationship is expressed liturgically and sacrificially.... The human person is *homo liturgicus*, created to glorify God through service, expressed as a sacrifice of praise.[2]

CREATION

The Garden is described as a sort of temple (where God meets with his human creatures), with Adam as Priest:

---

1. Hahn, "Canon, Cult and Covenant: The Promise of Liturgical Hermeneutics," in Bartholomew, *Canon and Biblical Interpretation*.
2. Hahn, "Canon, Cult and Covenant," 213.

> The LORD God took the man and put him in the garden of Eden to work it and keep it. (Gen 2:15)

> The author's intent [is] to depict creation as a fashioning of a cosmic temple, which, like the later tabernacle and Temple, would be a meeting place for God and the human person made in his image and likeness. . . . The biblical authors' intent [is] to describe creation as a royal temple building by a heavenly king. The human person in these pages is intentionally portrayed as a royal firstborn and high-priestly figure, a kind of priest-king set to rule as vice-regent over the temple-kingdom of creation.[3]

See also the similar treatments by Gregory Beale, *The Temple and the Church's Mission*; Allen Ross, *Recalling the Hope of Glory: Biblical Worship from the Garden to the New Creation*; Gordon J. Wenham, "Sanctuary Symbolism in the Garden of Eden Story," in *Proceedings of the Ninth World Congress of Jewish Studies, Division A: The Period of the Bible* (1986): 19–25).

> The first of God's mighty works then, the creation of the world, has a liturgical climax—the divine and human "rest" of the seventh day.[4]

FALL

The issue in the fall was an issue of worship (see chapter 2 above): the choice before Adam and Eve was: "Whom are you going to worship? Who is going to be in the center of your lives, on the throne of your hearts?" Paul describes their choice:

> Although they knew God, they did not honor him as God or give thanks to him. . . . They exchanged the truth about God for a lie and worshiped and served the creature rather than the Creator. (Rom 1:21, 25)

See also Ron Man, "False and True Worship in Romans 1," *Bibliotheca Sacra* 157 [Jan.-March 2000]:26–34.

> Adam's disobedience was understood inner-biblically as having something to do with a failure to offer himself—what we might call a failure of worship.[5]

---

3. Hahn, "Canon, Cult and Covenant," 213.
4. Hahn, "Canon, Cult and Covenant," 215.
5. Hahn "Canon, Cult and Covenant," 221.

FLOOD

In the flood, God preserves Noah and his family. Upon disembarking from the altar, Noah builds an altar, offers sacrifices, and worships:

> So Noah went out, and his sons and his wife and his sons' wives with him. Every beast, every creeping thing, and every bird, everything that moves on the earth, went out by families from the ark. Then Noah built an altar to the LORD and took some of every clean animal and some of every clean bird and offered burnt offerings on the altar. (Gen 8:18–20)

EXODUS

> As Adam was made to worship, God's chosen people are liberated expressly for worship.[6]

> Let my people go, that they might worship me." (Exod 7:16; 8:1,20; 9:1,13; 10:3)

> . . . my chosen people, the people whom I formed for myself that they might declare my praise. (Isa 43:20–21)

> When Israel went out from Egypt,
> the house of Jacob from a people of strange language,
> Judah became his sanctuary,
> Israel his dominion. (Ps 114:1–2)

> The exodus was begun with a liturgical act—the celebration of the Passover—and it "concludes" . . . with the construction of the tabernacle.[7]

THE LAW AND THE NATION OF ISRAEL

> Much of the Law, in fact, consists of regulations how God is to be rightly worshipped.[8]

---

6. Hahn, "Canon, Cult and Covenant," 215.
7. Hahn, "Canon, Cult and Covenant," 216.
8. Hahn, "Canon, Cult and Covenant," 216.

"You shall be to me a kingdom of priests and a holy nation." (Exod 19:6)

In fact, the reigns of both Judah's and Israel's kings in Kings and Chronicles are evaluated by the writer in each case as "(king's name) did *right* in the sight of the LORD" *or* "(king's name) did *evil* in the sight of the LORD"—and this always spoke to whether they worshipped Yahweh truly, or turned to idolatry; and, as their worship went, so went the nation's.

DAVID

David greatly developed the worship life of the nation, culminating in his preparations for the building of the Temple (which his son Solomon would ultimately build).

See the extensive development of this theme in Peter Leithart, *From Silence to Song: The Davidic Liturgical Revolution*.

> David's own thanksgiving hymn (1 Chr 16:7–36) is presented as a kind of paradigm for Israel's prayer. It is, in essence, a celebration of God's covenant in liturgical form. This hymn sets the tone and provides the content for the acts of worship and the theology of worship we find in the Psalter. God is praised and thanked in remembrance of his mighty works in creation and for his saving words and deeds in the life of Israel—the defining experience being that of the exodus and the covenant.[9]

> In the Temple worship, the precise sacrificial system of the Mosaic cult continues, but there are new elements and accents. The kingdom's corporate worship takes the form of praise and thanksgiving. Many commentators have identified the centrality of songs of praise and songs of thanksgiving in the Temple liturgy.[10]

> The Davidic kingdom marks the fullest expression of the Bible's liturgical anthropology [man created to worship] and teleology [worship goal/purpose] of the biblical revelation].[11]

---

9. Hahn, "Canon, Cult and Covenant," 219.
10. Hahn, "Canon, Cult and Covenant," 218–19.
11. Hahn, "Canon, Cult and Covenant," 218.

THE WORSHIP TRAJECTORY AND GOAL OF THE ENTIRE BIBLE

PSALMS AND PROPHETS

> We see in these psalms and in the prophetic literature a new and deepening understanding of the liturgical vocation of biblical man. In the prophets, this recognition of the inner truth of sacrifice often takes the form of denouncing the corruption of Israel's cult and worship (e.g. Isa 1:10–13; 66:2–4; Jer 7:21–24; Amos 4:4–5, 6b; Mic 6:6–8; Hos 6:6; Mal 1:10, 13–14). Positively, worship comes to be seen as a sacrificial offering in thanksgiving for redemption, for deliverance from death. Praise is revealed as the sacrifice by which men and women are to glorify God (Ps 50:14, 33; 141:2). God is portrayed as desiring that Israel serve him—not with the blood of animals but with their whole hearts, aligning their will with his, making their whole lives a sacrifice of praise and thanksgiving (Ps 40:6–8; 51:16–17). With this profound understanding that they are called to a pure worship of the heart comes the recognition that no amount of ethical striving or moral reform can make them holy enough to serve their God. A new covenant is promised as a new exodus and a new creation in which there will be a forgiveness of sins and a divine transformation of the heart (Jer 31:31–34; 32:40; Ezek 36:24–28).[12]

And so we see the significant worship trajectory of the Old Testament account. In part 4, chapter 1 we will see the culmination and fulfillment of this trajectory in the New Testament.

> The human person has been shown from the first pages of Genesis to the last of Revelation to be liturgical by nature, created and destined to live in the spiritual house of creation, as children of a royal and priestly family that offers sacrifices of praise to their Father-Creator with whom they dwell in a covenant of peace and love.... The story of the Bible is the story of humankind's journey to true worship in spirit and truth in the presence of God. That is the trajectory, the direction towards which narrative leads. This true worship is revealed to be the very purpose of God's creation in the beginning.[13]

[*Worship Notes* 16.7, August 2021]

---

12. Hahn, "Canon, Cult and Covenant," 219–20.
13. Hahn "Canon, Cult and Covenant," 225–26.

2

Important Themes in Old Testament Worship

WORSHIP AS *RESPONSE*

Response to *revelation* (Ps 150:2)

> God said to Moses, "I AM WHO I AM." And he said, "Say this to the people of Israel: 'I AM has sent me to you.'" God also said to Moses, "Say this to the people of Israel: 'The LORD, the God of your fathers, the God of Abraham, the God of Isaac, and the God of Jacob, has sent me to you.' This is my name forever, and thus I am to be remembered throughout all generations." (Exod 3:14–15; also 34:6–7; Rom 1:19–20)

Response to *redemption*

> God said, "But I will be with you, and this shall be the sign for you, that I have sent you: when you have brought the people out of Egypt, you shall serve [worship] God on this mountain." (Exod 3:12; also 6:6)

Response to *relationship* (covenant)

> "I will take you to be my people, and I will be your God, and you shall know that I am the LORD your God." (Exod 6:7; also 19:5)

Note: the phrase "the LORD our God" is used 440 times in the Old Testament, and "the LORD their God" 39 times: obviously a hugely important concept.

Response to *requirements*

> "You shall not make for yourself a carved image, or any likeness of anything that is in heaven above, or that is in the earth beneath, or that is in the water under the earth. You shall not bow down to them or serve them." (Exod 20:4–5; also entire book of Leviticus)

Again and again, the Old Testament makes the point that the Holy one can be approached only in the way that He Himself stipulates and makes possible.[1]

GOD'S GRACE, LOVINGKINDNESS, MERCY

This theme is contrary to a common misconception: that "the God of the Old Testament is a God of hate; the God of the New Testament is a God of love."
Rather, God's fundamental nature never changes:

> The LORD passed before him and proclaimed, "The LORD, the LORD, a God merciful and gracious, slow to anger, and abounding in steadfast love and faithfulness, keeping steadfast love for thousands, forgiving iniquity and transgression and sin." (Exod 34:6–7)

It is important to recognize that the sacrifices were not intended to earn salvation; they were the grateful offerings of an *already redeemed* people:

> The liturgies of Israel were God-given ordinances of grace, witnesses to grace. The sacrifice of lambs and bulls and goats were not ways of placating an angry God, currying favor with God as in the pagan worship of the Baalim. They were God-given covenantal witnesses to grace—that the God who alone could wipe out their sins would be gracious.[2]

1. Peterson, *Engaging with God*, 35.
2. James Torrance, *Worship, Community and the Triune God of Grace*, 60.

This concept is expressed most often in the Old Testament with the Hebrew word *ḥesed* (חֶסֶד), which is variously translated "steadfast love," "lovingkindness," "love," "mercy." The term speaks of God's *loyal love* to those in covenant with him; as such, it a close Old Testament parallel to the New Testament concept of "grace."

> Because your *steadfast love* is better than life, my lips will praise you. (Ps 63:3; see also Exod 34:6–7; Num 14:18; Deut 5:10; Ruth 1:8; 2 Sam 9:3; 1 Kgs 3:6; Ezra 9:9; Ps 23:6; 32:10; 136:1–26; 145:8; Jer 9:24)

The God of *both* testaments is a God of grace!

GOD'S INITIATIVE

God always acts first to reveal and show mercy and redeem (see part 2, chapter 1).

Examples: Adam and Eve hide from God, and God pursues *them*. Abraham is called by God while a pagan. Moses and David are both called by God while tending sheep. God breaks sovereignly into, and completely redirects, Paul's life while he is an attacker of the church.

CALLING ON THE NAME OF THE LORD

The phrase is used to denote both private and public acts of worship.

> To Seth also a son was born, and he called his name Enosh. At that time people began to *call upon the name of the Lord*. (Gen 4:26)

> From there Abraham moved to the hill country on the east of Bethel and pitched his tent, with Bethel on the west and Ai on the east. And there he built an altar to the LORD and called upon the name of the LORD. (Gen 12:8; also 13:4; 26:25; Psa 116:13,17; 1 Cor 1:2)

God *reveals* his name; *calling* on that name is a response of worship:

WORSHIP OF THE HEART

(see part 1, chapter 2, "Heart Worship")

[*Worship Notes* 6.9, September 2011; 6.10, October 2011]

3

The Supremacy of God's Name in the Old Testament

> You have exalted above all things your name and your word. (Ps 138:2)

> "I am the Lord; that is my name;
> my glory I give to no other."(Isa 42:8)

THE NATURE OF GOD'S NAME

As is well known, names in Scripture carry much more weight than mere appellation or identification: they speak of the character or reputation of the one so named; nowhere is this more true than in the case of God. J. Hampton Keathley suggests that "in Scripture, the names of God are like miniature portraits and promises."[1]

The many names and titles God gives himself in the Old Testament each says something important about his nature (e.g., *El Shaddai*, God Almighty, Gen 17:1–2; *El Elyon*, God Most High, Gen 14:18–19; etc.); most importantly, of course, he takes upon himself the special covenant name of *Yahweh* (Jehovah).[2]

---

1. Keathley, "Names of God."
2. It has been pointed out that all these and other descriptive names given to God

The common phrase "the name of the Lord" (and the worship response to "call on the name of the Lord"; see part 3, chapter 2) speaks of the totality of his glorious person, character, and reputation.

THE PURITY OF GOD'S NAME

> "You shall not take the name of the Lord your God in vain." (Exodus 20:7)

"Profane" in its original meaning is the opposite of "sacred," and refers to something intended for common (as opposed to religious) use: as in the distinction in the Old Testament between implements and vessels reserved [set apart, "holy"] for use in Tabernacle or Temple worship, as opposed to everyday objects. Hence "profanity" means a flippant or casual use of something meant for sacred purposes. The "name of the Lord," precisely because it speaks of his holy and majestic character, is unspeakably holy, and should never be used in any way other than in worship.

It has also been pointed out that, because as Christians we bear the very name of Christ, our behavior should likewise not be profane (this would be another way of taking God's name in vain); we should be "be holy, for I am holy" (Lev 11:44; 1 Pet 1:16).

GOD'S PASSION AND PURPOSE FOR HIS NAME

> God also said to Moses, "Say this to the people of Israel, 'The Lord, the God of your fathers, the God of Abraham, the God of Isaac, and the God of Jacob, has sent me to you.' This is my name forever, and thus I am to be remembered throughout all generations." (Exod 3:15)

> "But for this purpose I have raised you up, to show you my power, so that my name may be proclaimed in all the earth." (Exod 9:16)

> And he said, "I will make all my goodness pass before you and will proclaim before you my name 'The Lord.' And I will be gracious to whom I will be gracious, and will show mercy on whom I will show mercy." (Exod 33:19)

---

in the Old Testament are subsumed and fulfilled by Jesus, "the name that is above every name" (Phil 2:9).

"For the Lord will not forsake his people, for his great name's sake, because it has pleased the Lord to make you a people for himself." (1 Samuel 12:22)

"He [Solomon] shall build a house for my name, and I will establish the throne of his kingdom forever." (2 Sam 7:13)

Your name, O Lord, endures forever,
Your renown, O Lord, throughout all ages. (Ps 135:13)

You have exalted above all things
Your name and your word. (Ps 138:2)

"I am the Lord; that is my name;
my glory I give to no other,
nor my praise to carved idols." (Isa 42:8)

"For my own sake, for my own sake, I do it,
for how should my name be profaned?
My glory I will not give to another." (Isa 48:11)

"None of them cast away the detestable things their eyes feasted on, nor did they forsake the idols of Egypt. Then I said I would pour out my wrath upon them and spend my anger against them in the midst of the land of Egypt. But I acted for the sake of my name, that it should not be profaned in the sight of the nations among whom they lived, in whose sight I made myself known to them in bringing them out of the land of Egypt." (Ezek 20:8b-9)

"Therefore say to the house of Israel, Thus says the Lord God: It is not for your sake, O house of Israel, that I am about to act, but for the sake of my holy name, which you have profaned among the nations to which you came. And I will vindicate the holiness of my great name, which has been profaned among the nations, and which you have profaned among them." (Ezek 36:22-23)

"For from the rising of the sun to its setting my name will be great among the nations, and in every place incense will be offered to my name, and a pure offering." (Mal 1:11)

PART 3. OLD TESTAMENT STUDIES

CALLING UPON/ INVOKING GOD'S NAME

(See also part 3, chapter 2)

In trust/devotion

> To Seth also a son was born, and he called his name Enosh. At that time people began to call upon the name of the Lord. (Gen 4:26)

> From there [Abram] moved to the hill country on the east of Bethel and pitched his tent, with Bethel on the west and Ai on the east. And there he built an altar to the Lord and called upon the name of the Lord. (Gen 12:8)

> So [Isaac] built an altar there and called upon the name of the Lord and pitched his tent there. (Gen 26:25)

> Some trust in chariots and some in horses
> but we trust in the name of the Lord our God. (Ps 20:7)

> Our help is in the name of the Lord,
> who made heaven and earth. (Ps 124:8)

> The name of the Lord is a strong tower;
> the righteous man runs into it and is safe. (Prov 18:10)

> "For at that time I will change the speech of the peoples to a pure speech, that all of them may call upon the name of the Lord and serve him with one accord." (Zeph 3:9)

In praise/thanksgiving

> For I will proclaim the name of the Lord; ascribe greatness to our God! (Deut 32:3)

> Oh give thanks to the Lord; call upon his name;
> make known his deeds among the peoples! (1 Chr 16:8; Ps 105:1)

> And [Job] said, "Naked I came from my mother's womb, and naked shall I return.
> The Lord gave, and the Lord has taken away;
> blessed be the name of the Lord." (Job 1:21)

> Blessed be the name of the Lord
> from this time forth and forevermore!
> From the rising of the sun to its setting,
> the name of the Lord is to be praised! (Ps 113:2–3)

> I will offer to you the sacrifice of thanksgiving
> and call on the name of the Lord. (Ps 116:17)

> Let them praise the name of the Lord!
> For he commanded and they were created. (Ps 148:5)

> And you will say in that day:
> "Give thanks to the Lord, call upon his name,
> make known his deeds among the peoples,
> proclaim that his name is exalted." (Isa 12:4)

> Therefore in the east give glory to the Lord;
> in the coastlands of the sea, give glory to the name of the Lord,
> the God of Israel. (Isa 24:15)

In petition/blessing

> "And you call upon the name of your god, and I will call upon the name of the Lord, and the God who answers by fire, he is God." (1 Kgs 18:24)

> And when David had finished offering the burnt offerings and the peace offerings, he blessed the people in the name of the Lord. (1 Chr 16:2)

> Then I called on the name of the Lord:
> "O Lord, I pray, deliver my soul!" (Ps 116:4)

> And it shall come to pass that everyone who calls on the name of the Lord shall be saved. (Joel 2:32)

[*Worship Notes* 8.4, April 2013]

4

The Psalms
Israel's Hymnbook ... and Ours

THE UNIQUENESS OF THE PSALMS

The Psalms hold a unique place in both Jewish and Christian piety.

> Psalms are the language we use when we need a voice other than our own.[1]

> The Psalms convey the whole range of human emotion, from despondent sorrow (Psalm 88) to ecstatic joy (Psalm 47 or 48), from ravaging guilt (Psalm 51) to profound gratitude (Psalm 136). In Calvin's famous phrase, the Psalms are "the anatomy of the soul." They teach us that with the God of the covenant, no human emotion is out of place in prayer.[2]

In the fourth century A.D. the great theologian Athanasius wrote:

> Elsewhere in the Bible you read only that the Law commands this or that to be done, you listen to the Prophets to learn about the Savior's coming or you turn to the historical books to learn the doings of the kings and holy men; but in the Psalter, besides all these things, you learn about *yourself*. You find depicted in it all

---

1. Plantinga and Rozeboom, 160.
2. Witvliet, *The Biblical Psalms in Christian Worship*, 30.

> the movements of your soul, all its changes, its ups and downs, its failures and recoveries.[3]

> It is reported that Athanasius, an outstanding Christian leader of the fourth century, declared that the Psalms have a unique place in the Bible because most of Scripture speaks *to us*, while the Psalms speak *for us*.[4]

> The Psalms have among other roles in Scripture one which is peculiarly their own: to touch and kindle us rather than simply to address us.[5]

The psalmists are profoundly honest before God. Sometimes they are praising God for his profound blessings; often they are crying out in confusion, frustration and even anger at God for his seeming indifference or absence (though, with the sole exception of Psalm 88, every Psalm like this turns back to hope in God by the end). We find company and comfort here in the midst of the realities of our human experience, seeing that others have gone, and felt, that way before; and yet they learned, and invite us, to taste and see that the Lord is good.

With their profound honesty the psalmists not only give us words to express our most weighty feelings, but also thereby form our own language of praise and prayer.

> Every man on every occasion can find in it Psalms which fit his needs, which he feels to be as appropriate as if they had been set there just for his sake. In no other book can he find words to equal them, nor better words.[6]

C. S Lewis commented on the profound spirituality of the Psalmists:

> I want to stress what I think that we (or at least I) need more [than instruction about sacrifice]; the joy and delight in God which meet us in the Psalms. . . . These poets knew far less reason than we for loving God. They did not know that He offered them eternal joy; still less that He would die to win it for them. Yet they express a longing for Him, for His mere presence, which comes only to the

---

3. Athanasius, *On the Incarnation*, quoted in Witvliet, *The Biblical Psalms in Christian Worship*, 7. Emphasis added.

4. Bernhard Anderson, *Out of the Depths*, x. Emphases added.

5. Kidner, *Psalms 1–72*, 28.

6. Luther, "Preface to the Psalms," quoted in Witvliet, *The Biblical Psalms in Christian Worship*, 40.

best Christians or to Christians in their best moments. They long to live all their days in the Temple so that they may constantly see "the fair beauty of the LORD" (Ps 27:4). Their longing to go up to Jerusalem and "appear before the presence of God" is like a physical thirst (42:1–2). From Jerusalem His presence flashes out "in perfect beauty" (50:2). Lacking that encounter with Him, their souls are parched like a waterless countryside (63:1). They crave to be "satisfied with the pleasures" of His house (65:4). Only there can they be at ease, like a bird in the nest (84:3; 84:1–2). One day of those "pleasures" is better than a lifetime spent elsewhere 84:10, 11, 12).[7]

AUTHORS AND FORMS OF THE PSALMS

David wrote 73 of the Psalms; the "Sons of Korah" wrote 11; Solomon, David's son, wrote 2; Asaph wrote 2 ("Asaph was the chief" of the Levites that King David appointed to be "ministers before the ark of the LORD, to invoke, to thank, and to praise the LORD, the God of Israel," 1 Chr 16:4–5); men named Heman and Ethan wrote 1 each; and the authors of 49 of the Psalms are not identified.

There are a wide variety of types of the Psalms, used in quite different ways: from private, personal prayers to God (whether of praise or despair) to formal, public ones of praise. Some of the identified types include: Salvation History Psalms, Laments (Community and Individual), Songs of Thanksgiving, Hymns of Praise, Festival Songs and Liturgies, Songs of Trust and Meditation.

Some of David's struggles take on the form of predictive Messianic prophecy, such as Psalm 22 ("My God, my God, why have you forsaken me?"); and he also provides a beloved expression of faith and trust in Psalm 23 ("The LORD is my Shepherd, I shall not want"). He created a profound and lasting vehicle for personal confession in Psalm 51 (after his sin with Bathsheba was exposed: "Have mercy on me, O God, according to your steadfast love; according to your abundant mercy blot out my transgressions"), as well as a moving expression of received forgiveness in Psalm 32 ("Blessed is the one whose transgression is forgiven, whose sin is covered").

David and the other Psalmists walked with God, and lived out the ups and downs of that walk in conversation with their Lord; we can read of that

---

7. Lewis, *Reflections on the Psalms*, 50–51.

interaction, and find expression for our own pilgrimage in the words they have left for us.

HOW GOD IS REPRESENTED IN THE PSALMS

God's Powerful Protection

Kenneth Bailey has observed that Psalm 18:1–3 piles up a number of attributes and metaphors that are common throughout the Psalms, all of them what he calls "homeland security" images.[8] Hence:

> I love you, O LORD, my strength.
> The LORD is my rock and my fortress and my deliverer,
> my God, my rock, in whom I take refuge,
> my shield, and the horn of my salvation, my stronghold.
> I call upon the LORD, who is worthy to be praised,
> and I am saved from my enemies.

In an often hostile and barren environment where bandits and invading armies were a regular threat, the Jewish people's dependence upon God's promised watchcare was an important part of their walk of worship.

God's Gentle Care

Bailey points out, though, that perhaps to balance this perspective and avoid a sort of "siege mentality," the people of God are presented in the Psalms also with "three countercultural options for understanding the nature of God." These are the images of God being like a *shepherd* (Ps 23; 28:9; 78:71–72; 80:1; see also the people of God represented as "sheep" in 74:1; 78:52; 79:13; 95:7; 100:3); God being like a *father* (68:5; 89:26; 103:13; see also 27:10); and God being like a *mother* (131:2; see also 27:10; Isa 66:12–13). God is a God of compassion and care. Bailey adds: "It is no accident that the trilogy of parables in Luke 15:1–31 centers on a good shepherd, a good woman, and a good father."[9]

---

8. Bailey, *Good Shepherd*, 35–36.
9. Bailey, *The Good* Shepherd, 36–37.

God's Loyal Love

The people of Israel were the blessed beneficiaries (though not always tuned into it) of God's *ḥesed*, a Hebrew word that gives a beautiful and many-faceted description of God's character in relationship to this people. The word refers to his "loyal love," to his faithfulness towards those who are bound to him (and he to them) in covenant; and is variously translated in English "lovingkindness," "mercy," "steadfast love."

The term is used of God 249 times in the Old Testament, and 127 times in Psalms alone. God is a covenant-keeping God! 26 of the occurrences in Psalms are in Psalm 136, where every verse ends with the same refrain. Obviously this Psalm was used in the public worship of Israel, where the priest would recite the first line of every verse, such as in verse 1:

> Give thanks to the LORD, for he is good,

and the congregation would respond, in each instance:

> for his steadfast love [*ḥesed*] endures forever!

In the first line of each pair the priest gives a beginning doxology (verses 1–3), traces God's work in creation (4–9), recounts his mighty redeeming acts in the Exodus from Egypt (10–16), rehearses his continuing faithfulness to his chosen people through their history (17–25), and then gives a concluding doxology (26)—after each line the people responding with the refrain about God's never-ending *ḥesed*. This participatory act allowed the people to participate in declaring God's praise in the corporate assembly; and the formative nature of this practice for young and old alike was the unmistakable reminder that the Lord's "steadfast love endures forever"!

THE POETRY OF THE PSALMS

In Hebrew poetry the lines are not arranged in strict metrical patterns, such as is the case in most Western poetic expressions; much less are there regular rhyme schemes. Rather the stylistic distinctive of the Psalms is the use of *parallelism* between pairs of lines: the second line offering an idea similar to the first (called "synonymous parallelism"; or a contrasting idea ("antithetical parallelism"); or a development and extension of the idea ("synthetic parallelism"). The most remarkable thing about this poetic structure of the

Psalms is that it lends itself to translation into other languages in a way that rhyming or line meter would never allow for. C. S. Lewis wrote:

> It is . . . a wise provision of God's, that poetry which was to be turned into all languages should have as its chief formal characteristic one that does not disappear (as mere metre does) in translation.[10]

And Kidner similarly points out:

> This type of poetry loses less than perhaps any other in the process of translation. In many literatures the appeal of a poem lies chiefly in verbal felicities and associations, or in metrical language. But the poetry of the Psalms has a broad simplicity of rhythm and imagery which survives transplanting into almost any soil. Above all, the fact that its parallelisms are those of sense rather than of sound allows it to reproduce its chief effects with very little loss of either force or beauty. It is well fitted by God's providence to invite all the earth to sing the glory of his name.[11]

God intended these Psalms to find full expression in our vernacular, that we might read and sing them to his praise!

THE CLIMACTIC DOXOLOGY

The last Psalms, 146–150, all begin and end with the same familiar Hebrew phrase, which has found its way into the Christian vocabulary of every language: *Hallelu-jah*. It is comprised of two words, a plural command to "praise," and its direct object *Jah*, short for *Jahweh*, the covenant name for God in the Old Testament. It is important to note that Hallelujah is not an interjection of praise (as we often use it), but rather a corporate *command* or *invitation* to praise.

Psalm 150 not only begins and ends with that phrase, but the same verb is used at least twice in each of its 6 verses, 13 times in all. As such, the Psalm's resounding call serves as a concluding Doxology to the entire book of Psalms, summarizing the book's overarching call to *praise the Lord*. God's praise is to be declared with instruments (trumpet, lute, harp, tambourine, cymbals) and with dance, as well as by "everything that has breath."

---

10. Lewis, *Reflections on the Psalms*, 12.
11. Kidner, *Psalms 1–72*, 4.

It is often pointed out that, unlike many contemporary songs of praise that just string together unsupported emotive cries of praise, the psalmists almost always give reasoned grounds for giving praise to God: because of his works of creation, his attributes, his acts in history (especially the history of the nation of Israel). So too in Psalm 150, Israel (and we) are instructed to "praise him *according to* his excellent greatness" (v. 2b)—God has revealed and demonstrated his excellent greatness, and we are to praise him accordingly. "Great is the Lord, and [therefore] greatly to be praised" (Psalm 96:4): here is an inescapable connection between God's self-revelation and the appropriate response of worship. Hence the utter appropriateness of reciting God's Word in balance with singing in our corporate services.

CONCLUSION

The Psalms are a precious gift from God to his people; each of them gives us a little different angle from which to view God and worship him. There can never be too many ways to do that!

[*Worship Notes* 7.10, October 2012]

5

Is "God Inhabits the Praises of His People" Really Biblical?

by Zac Hicks[1]

I reluctantly lift up the truce-flag of exegetical honesty. I desperately want it to say it. Many worship leaders (including myself) have quoted it as saying it. It would be a great proof-text-style summary verse for a very important aspect of the theology of worship. But the fact is that the translational evidence leans heavily against us being able to say that "God inhabits the praises of his people" is an accurate rendering of the Hebrew of Psalm 22:3. Now, it is certainly a possible translation, but it is not the one that makes the best sense of the poetry. Before we unpack this, let's look at why it would be so valuable for it to say what it doesn't say.

WHY I WISH IT SAYS WHAT IT DOESN'T SAY

This verse, for worship leaders, is akin to that elusive "one verse" that proof-texts the Trinity for many Christians. It's an exegetical silver bullet. "God inhabits the praises of his people" is a one-stop shop articulation of the core of Christian worship: that God chooses to manifest himself uniquely in the context of gathered, corporate worship generally and perhaps in

---

1. Many thanks to Zac Hicks for his permission to include in this collection this intriguing blog post of his (posted on January 24, 2012 on zachicks.com).

the singing[2] of God's people particularly. In an effort to elevate singing to nearly "sacramental" status (many have observed that evangelicals [probably due in part to the influence of Pentecostal theology on the whole of evangelicalism] have made congregational singing the "third sacrament" of Protestantism because of how much weight we give to experiencing God's presence in the midst of singing), this verse would be a slam dunk argument in less than ten words.

Does God really inhabit the praises of his people? You better believe it. We would just need to work a little harder and ponder Scripture more broadly and systematically to unearth this rich theological/doxological truth. Psalm 22:3 just doesn't say it as clearly as we would hope.

WHY IT PROBABLY DOESN'T SAY WHAT I WISH IT WOULD SAY

Hebrew poetry is different than English poetry. Typically, English poems use rhyme at the ends of phrases alongside other wonderful poetic devices, but Hebrew poetry was more often concerned with other elements of style, like balanced metrical patterns. Hebrew meter is often defined by "units" (not necessarily syllables) in how meter is counted and added up. A phrase which groups these units is called a "colon"—one line of poetry. Two lines paired together are called "bicola," while three grouped lines are called "tricola." Scholars will often shorthand syllables and cola with little equations like this (Psalm 22:1, 12):[3]

> (1) My God, my God, why have You forsaken me?
> My moaning is of the distance of my salvation! (4+4)
> (12) Don't be distant from me,
> for trouble is near;
> there is certainly no helper! (2+2+2)

Verse 1's equation reads "4+4," meaning, "there are four (Hebrew, not English) units in the first line and four units in the second line of this bicola." Verse 12's equation reads "2+2+2," meaning, "there are two units in each of the three lines of this tricola."

---

2. The Hebrew word for "praises" (*tehillah*) is used elsewhere (e.g. the inscription of Psalm 145) to mean, quite particularly, "praise-songs" or "hymns."

3. This translation is from Peter Craigie, *Psalms* 1–50, 194.

All this is important to the translational debate surrounding 22:3. This verse is a bicola, but the question is whether it is 3+2 or 2+3. In this five-unit bicola, the word in the middle could either be grammatically tied to the first colon (making it 3+2) or the second colon (making it 2+3). The middle word is *yoshev*, the verb for "sit, dwell, inhabit." Various translations will render *yoshev* as "inhabit" (KJV) or "enthrone" (NIV, NASB, ESV). If *yoshev* were part of the first colon, the translation would be something like:

> You are enthroned as holy; (3)
> The praise of Israel. (2)

If *yoshev* were a part of the second colon, the translation would be something like:

> You are holy; (2) Inhabiting/enthroned on the praises of Israel. (3)

Hopefully, even in somewhat straightened English, you can see the difference in meaning depending on where the key verb fits. Either is plausible. How do we decide?

John Goldingay, siding with the translation of the Septuagint (LXX, the Greek translation of the Hebrew Bible) and Jerome's Vulgate, offers what is to me a convincing case that the former 3+2 rendering should be preferred over the latter:

> The idea of Yhwh's sitting enthroned in the heavens or in Zion is a familiar one (2:4; 55:19 [20]; 80:1 [2]; 99:1; 123:1; cf. 99:1–3 for the association with Yhwh's being the holy one; also Isa 57:15). Likewise, the idea that Yhwh as Israel's praise is a familiar one (Deut 10:21; Jer 17:14), but the idea of Yhwh's being enthroned on or inhabiting Israel's praise is unparalleled, and if either of these is the psalm's point, one might have expected it to be expressed more clearly. The fact that 3–2 is the more common line division supports the conclusion that LXX construes the line correctly.[4]

In other words, two things stand out:

1. The content of the 3+2 rendering is more "normal" for the way Scripture talks about God elsewhere. (God as "enthroned Holy One" is a common attribution, whereas God "inhabiting/enthroned on Israel's praises" is an utterly unique phrase.)
2. 3+2 is apparently more common than 2+3.

4. Goldingay, *Psalms*, 327–28.

This argument isn't airtight. It's just sensible, given the data. It's still possible that the other translational option is correct, but it is less reasonable. If I'm honest, I really want to believe the less reasonable option, but if I'm truthful, it's not the best choice. So while it doesn't seal the deal, the "reasonable doubt" I now have leads me to not want to misquote Scripture. Here I side with the NIV and Goldingay (and Jerome and LXX), over against great translations and scholars like the NASB, ESV, and Peter Craigie.

LEADING WITH RIGOROUS INTEGRITY

Why have I taken so much time to dissect Hebrew minutiae on a blog post? Ultimately, it comes down to integrity. Will I approach the Scriptures as honestly as possible, and will I model that honesty thoroughly before the people I lead, even when it eliminates what I considered a major tool in my "worship theology shorthand" arsenal? Sometimes (and I am guilty of this, too), we allow a little mis-exegesis to slide because "it's just too good." But if we desire to be trustworthy as pastors, teachers, and leaders, we need to try to be as exegetically honest as possible, even as Christ forgives and washes His blood over all our shoddy best efforts.

(By the way, how did I come up with this? Do I sit around reading my Hebrew Bible? No way. The punchline of this little exercise is that, upon seeing so many varying translations of this key verse, I decided to dive into the Hebrew, aiming at proving the validity of "God enthroned on the praises of His people." Quite the opposite occurred, much to my chagrin.)

PART 4

New Testament Studies

1

The Worship Trajectory and Goal of the Entire Bible
Part 2: New Testament

Scott Hahn, in the article referenced in part 3, chapter 1, shows how each major movement in the Old Testament culminates in worship. Now we will continue on to see this pattern reflected also in the New Testament completion of the Bible's worship trajectory.

> The human person has been shown from the first pages of Genesis to the last of Revelation to be liturgical by nature, created and destined to live in the spiritual house of creation, as children of a royal and priestly family that offers sacrifices of praise to their Father-Creator with whom they dwell in a covenant of peace and love. . . . The story of the Bible is the story of humankind's journey to true worship in spirit and truth in the presence of God. That is the trajectory, the direction towards which narrative leads. This true worship is revealed to be the very purpose of God's creation in the beginning.[1]

CHRIST

Even though Adam and Eve "knew God, they did not honor him as God or give thanks to him . . . [and they] worshiped and served the creature rather

---

1. Hahn, "Canon, Cult and Covenant," 225–26.

than the Creator" (Rom 1:21,25). Christ, on the other hand, passes the test which Adam and Eve failed:

> "It is written:
> 'You shall worship the Lord your God,
> and him only shall you serve.'" (Matt 4:10)

(On this theme, see also part 2, chapter 2)

Paul further develops this contrast in Romans 5:12–20:

> For as by the one man's disobedience the many were made sinners, so by the one man's obedience the many will be made righteous. (5:19)

And in 1 Corinthians 15:45–49, Paul even calls Christ "the last Adam":

> The first man Adam became a living being; the last Adam became a life-giving spirit. (15:45)

> Unlike Adam, who was made in the image of God, Christ did not grasp at equality with God, but instead offered his life in humility and obedience to God [Phil 2:6–8]. . . . Christ's self-offering is the worship expected originally of Adam and again of Israel as God's firstborn, royal and priestly people. His sacrifice marked the fulfillment of all that Israel's sacrificial system was intended to prepare and instruct Israel for—that through Israel all the nations of the world might learn to make a perfect offering of heart and will to God.[2]

Hahn also sees a fulfillment in Christ of the Exodus theme of the Old Testament:

> The New Testament writers appropriate the Old Testament understanding of the purpose for the exodus. . . . God's liberation of Israel was ordered to a very specific end—namely the establishment of Israel as God's royal and priestly people destined to glorify him among the nations.
>
> Echoes of that exodus purpose are clearly heard in Zechariah's canticle at the outset of Luke's Gospel (1: 67–79). In a song resounding with exodus imagery, Zechariah sees the "goal" of Christ's exodus [Luke 9:31] as precisely that of the first exodus—to

---

2. Hahn, "Canon, Cult and Covenant," 221–22.

establish . . . a holy and righteous people that worships in God's presence.[3]

THE CHURCH

The Church is described by Peter with terms and functions highly reminiscent of Israel:

> You yourselves like living stones are being built up as a spiritual house, to be a holy priesthood, to offer spiritual sacrifices acceptable to God through Jesus Christ. . . . But you are a chosen race, a royal priesthood, a holy nation, a people for his own possession, that you may proclaim the excellencies of him who called you out of darkness into his marvelous light. (1 Pet 2:5, 9)

Similar to Israel (though of course with some key differences), the church is a "people whom I formed for myself that they might declare my praise" (Isa 43:21). And the members of this new people of God are to live a lifestyle of worship, in continuity with and fulfillment of (now with the Spirit's help, Rom 8:4) the expectations of the Old Covenant:

> I appeal to you therefore, brethren, by the mercies of God, to present your bodies as a living sacrifice, holy and acceptable to God, which is your spiritual worship. (Rom 12:1)

> For God has done what the law, weakened by the flesh, could not do. By sending his own Son in the likeness of sinful flesh and for sin, he condemned sin in the flesh, in order that the righteous requirement of the law might be fulfilled in us, who walk not according to the flesh but according to the Spirit. (Rom 8:3–4)

THE REVELATION OF JOHN

We see in the concluding book of the Bible the trajectory towards faithful worship of the Creator God completed (not without many scenes of final rebellion, however). The worship of which God alone is worthy, and which was denied him in the fall (Rom 1:25), is finally consummated around the throne of God. We see the great scenes of worship in Revelation 4, 5, 7

---

3. Hahn, "Canon, Cult and Covenant," 222–23.

and 19, where God is surrounded by amazing angelic beings, "myriads of myriads" of angels (5:11), the redeemed from "every tribe and language and people and nation" (5:9; 7:9), and indeed all of creation (5:13), who are all exclaiming the praises of God and of the Lamb:

> "To him who sits on the throne and to the Lamb
> be blessing and honor and glory and might forever and ever!" (5:13)

Thus is the call of the gospel fulfilled:

> Then I saw another angel flying directly overhead, with an eternal gospel to proclaim to those who dwell on earth, to every nation and tribe and language and people. And he said with a loud voice, "Fear God and give him glory, because the hour of his judgment has come, and worship him who made heaven and earth, the sea and the springs of water." (14:6–7)

And, tellingly, Hahn states:

> At the conclusion of our liturgical reading of the canon, we hear the purpose and meaning of the entire Bible summed up in the refrain of the Apocalypse: "Worship God!" (Rev 19:20; 22:9).[4]

With little two words, in the very last chapter of the Bible, the angel summarizes for us what is indeed the call of the entire Bible: "Worship God!" (22:9).

[*Worship Notes* 16.8, September 2021]

---

4. Hahn, "Canon, Cult and Covenant," 225.

2

Important Themes in New Testament Worship

INWARD WORSHIP

(See the treatment of this crucial theme for both Old *and* New Testament worship in part 1, chapter 2: "Heart Worship.")

WHOLE-LIFE WORSHIP

(See the treatment of this theme in part 1, chapter 2: "Whole-Life Worship.")

ACCESS

The Old Covenant system of worship, in spite of its gracious provisions for relating to the covenant-keeping God of Israel (through a temporary covering of sin, in anticipation of Christ's atoning work, Rom 3:24–25), nevertheless was a system that demonstrated strongly the distance that sin had put between God and even his own chosen people. Access to the presence of God (represented in the architecture of the Tabernacle/Temple) was severely proscribed. The common people were allowed to enter only the courtyard of the Tabernacle/Temple; one had to be a priest to enter the Holy Place; while entry into the Holy of Holies was reserved for the high priest alone, who himself could enter only once a year, on the Day of Atonement (see Lev 16).

The book of Hebrews clearly demonstrates how all the barriers of this Old Covenant system were destroyed, and the way into the presence of God made fully available, by the redeeming death of Christ on the cross. That opening of the way into God's presence is powerfully dramatized by the tearing from top to bottom of the veil in the Jerusalem temple (the one barring access into the Holy of Holies, i.e., into the presence of God) at the precise moment of Christ's death (Matt 27:51; Mark 15:38; Luke 23:45). The way into the presence of God was now open by the removal of the barrier of sin by the perfect sacrifice of Christ.

In Hebrews 10:19–22 the author climactically turns to make application of the tremendous truths he has been expounding concerning the superiority of Christ, his priesthood, his sacrifice, and the New Covenant instituted by his atoning death. And so he declares:

> *Therefore*, brethren, since we have confidence to enter the holy places by the blood of Jesus, by the new and living way that he opened for us through the curtain, that is, through his flesh, and since we have a great priest over the house of God, *let us draw near* with a true heart in full assurance of faith, with our hearts sprinkled clean from an evil conscience and our bodies washed with pure water.

Note that the main verb of the sentence does not show up until verse 22; it is an imperative: we are to "draw near." The Greek verb (*proserchomai*) is one used commonly in the Septuagint (the Greek translation of the Old Testament) to speak of the approach to God in worship—though it was not really that "near" because of the restrictions of the Tabernacle/Temple setup, as seen above. But now that approach is clear and open and direct because of Christ's ministry; and so we are urged to come close "in full assurance of faith" and in the "confidence" we can have because of what Christ has accomplished for us. The writer is saying: you have this wonderful access through Christ (as he been explaining for 10 chapters)—now take full advantage of it! Enjoy to the fullest the advantages that are yours because of the superior benefits of the New Covenant.

(For more on our access to God through our Mediator, Jesus Christ, please see part 5, chapter 2.)

IMPORTANT THEMES IN NEW TESTAMENT WORSHIP

FREEDOM OF FORM

The New Testament is virtually silent on the matter of form for the church's worship. D. A. Carson goes so far as to say: "There is no single passage in the New Testament that establishes a paradigm for corporate worship."[1] And John Piper makes this astounding observation:

> In the New Testament, all the focus is on the reality of the glory of Christ, not the shadow and copy of religious objects and forms. It is stunning how indifferent the New Testament is to such things: there is no authorization in the New Testament for worship buildings, or worship dress, or worship times, or worship music, or worship liturgy or worship size or thirty-five-minute sermons, or Advent poems or choirs or instruments or candles. . . . Almost every worship tradition we have is culturally shaped rather than Biblically commanded.[2]

This is surprising, to say the least. The apostle Paul, for instance, writes letters to newly-established churches, and we would reasonably expect (even hope) that Paul would lay out specific and detailed instructions for these churches' worship (and hence for ours also). Yet that is exactly what he does *not* do. In fact, Gordon Fee observes that "what comes to us does so for the most part in the form of correction [for instance in 1 Cor 14]. We simply do not know enough to make far-reaching, all-inclusive statements about the nature of worship in the Pauline churches."[3]

It is a fair assumption that the non-specificity of the New Testament as to worship forms is intended by God to allow a great deal of flexibility and latitude as to specific structures for corporate worship. Piper suggests that we are "free to find place and time and dress and size and music and elements and objects that help us orient radically toward the supremacy of God in Christ."[4]

Of course, that freedom has also led to the worship debates that are so common in our day. If the Scriptures laid out as detailed a prescription for worship as we find in the Old Testament, there would be hardly any room for debate for churches that desired to be biblically faithful; but it is the latitude allowed that leaves room for differing opinions and (often) conflict.

---

1. Carson, "Worship under the Word," in Carson, *Worship by the Book*, 55.
2. Piper, "Our High Priest is The Son of God Perfect Forever."
3. Fee, *God's Empowering Presence*, 884 n. 13.
4. Piper, "Our High Priest is The Son of God Perfect Forever."

At the root of most of the current worship debates is the nature of the interface of worship and culture in the context in which a local church finds itself. It is incumbent upon the leaders of individual congregations to study the Scriptures, but also their culture and their congregation, and then to prayerfully make decisions about the form that worship will take in their particular church context. Bryan Chapell agrees:

> I think it behooves sessions [elder boards] . . . to discern what is the vision and mission of this church, and then to lock arms and say what is our mission. . . . Now, that means you have to be able to exegete culture too, I think, and not say just that our preferences are going to rule. . . . But principles of worship continue not to be discussed; much more preferences.[5]

(Much more on this complex subject in part 8: "Worship and Culture.")

[*Worship Notes* 4.4 (April 2009)/1.11 (November 2006); 4.5 (May 2009)/1.10 (October 2006); 4.6 (June 2009); 4.3 (March 2009)]

---

5. Chapell, "Profile of Today's Evangelical Church."

3

"Not Far From The Kingdom"
Seeing Things God's Way (Mark 12:28–34)

Here's a rarity in the gospels: a scribe coming to Jesus with an honest question! Far more often, the scribes and the other Jewish leaders are trying to criticize, entrap, or trick Jesus (cf. 12:13 in this very chapter), and turn the people away from him.

EXTERNAL PRACTICE

The scribes and Pharisees are of course also the object of Jesus' most scathing denunciations (see the whole of Matthew 23, and here in Mark 12:38). Jesus condemns them especially for the externality of their religion: practicing their rites for public view (Matthew 6:1–6; 23:27–28).

God always detests mere externality of practice without internal reality. Usually when we think of worship in the Old Testament, our thoughts go first to the rituals, ceremonies, and sacrifices of the Mosaic system; yet there is clear testimony throughout the Old Testament of the priority God places on the worship of the heart (see part 1, chapter 2: "Heart Worship"). In the prophets God criticizes the people for the very sacrifices he had himself commanded of them, because they were going through the motions without a true heart of devotion to him. As C.S. Lewis pointed out, it is not "that he really needed the blood of bulls and goats;"[1] he wanted the outward sacrifices to be an outward expression of an inward reality.

INTERNAL REALITY

In Mark 12 we see a stark contrast to the usual challenging and critical approach of the scribes to Jesus.

> And one of the scribes came up and heard them disputing with one another, and seeing that he answered them well, asked him, "Which commandment is the most important of all?"
>
> Jesus answered, "The most important is, 'Hear, O Israel: The Lord our God, the Lord is one. And you shall love the Lord your God with all your heart and with all your soul and with all your mind and with all your strength.' The second is this: 'You shall love your neighbor as yourself.' There is no other commandment greater than these."
>
> And the scribe said to him, "You are right, Teacher." (28–32a)

In a way, this is quite humorous: of course he's right, he's Jesus!!

The scribe is not taken aback by Jesus' answer (as so often the Jewish leaders were by Jesus' responses), but rather fully endorses Jesus' point of view. And then the scribe goes on to add this profound commentary on the significance of the two Great Commandments that Jesus has just cited:

> "You have truly said that he is one, and there is no other besides him. And to love him with all the heart and with all the understanding and with all the strength, and to love one's neighbor as oneself, is much more than all whole burnt offerings and sacrifices." (32b–33)

Often in the gospels we find the people marveling in wonder at the things Jesus does and the things he says: they are amazed at the power and wisdom of God working through him (see, for example, Matt 8:27; 9:33; Mark 12:17). But on a very few occasions we find Jesus himself marveling at the work of God in someone else's heart, for example in the heart of the Roman centurion:

> When Jesus heard this, he marveled and said to those who followed him, "Truly, I tell you, with no one in Israel have I found such faith." (Matt 8:10)

---

1. Lewis, "On Church Music," 98.

"NOT FAR FROM THE KINGDOM"

And here in Mark 12, Jesus commends the scribe's deep spiritual understanding:

> And when Jesus saw that he answered wisely, he said to him, "You are not far from the kingdom of God." (34a)

What a commendation indeed! Why is the scribe not far from the kingdom? Because the scribe is *looking at things the way God does*; he has a spiritual perspective in keeping with kingdom values. He sees the spiritual priority of love for God and for neighbor over all outward expressions of worship.

One can only wish Mark had told us what happened with the scribe, whether in fact he became a believer in and follower of Jesus. It seems likely, because of the spiritual trajectory he was already on, which Jesus himself identifies. This is surely a sign that the Holy Spirit was at work in his heart, showing him this most important of spiritual realities.

[*Worship Notes* 14.12, December 2019)

4

Worship and the Fall in Romans 1

Sometimes, when students at the schools I visit overseas learn that I have come to teach a course on worship, they ask questions like: "A whole course on worship?? What's he going to talk about for a whole week (or even two)?" But they soon see, as we delve deeply into the biblical text, what a far-reaching, overarching, and indeed central theme worship is in the Bible. The implications of a true scriptural understanding of worship are enormous, infusing from beginning to end the entire biblical story, and indeed all of human history.

Crucial to this perspective is Romans 1:18–25, where (as one author has put it) Paul has provided a "theological commentary on Genesis 3": in other words, Genesis 3 tells us what *happened*; Romans 1 tells us what it *means*. Paul's great exposition in Romans of the saving work of God through Christ is put by him in the context of the fall: laying out the blackness of human sin so that the glory of God's grace might shine all the more brightly.

The New Testament scholar Morna D. Hooker[1] has convincingly demonstrated that in Romans 1, Paul is not just talking about mankind in general, but Adam and Eve in particular: the linguistic and conceptual similarities between Genesis 3 and Romans 1 demonstrate that Paul is indeed speaking of our first parents in his portrayal of humanity's fallenness.

---

1. Hooker, "Adam in Romans 1," 297–306; "A Further Note on Romans 1," 181–83.

WORSHIP AND THE FALL IN ROMANS 1

> For what can be known about God is plain to them, because God has shown it to them. For his invisible attributes, namely, his eternal power and divine nature, have been clearly perceived, ever since the creation of the world, in the things that have been made. So they are without excuse. (Rom 1:19–20)

God clearly revealed himself to Adam and Eve; "his eternal power and divine nature" were "clearly perceived." In keeping with how he has always dealt with mankind, God himself initiated the relationship with Adam and Eve and revealed himself to them. They were "without excuse" because their rebellion could not be traced to a lack of knowledge of God and what he demanded.

> For although they knew God, they did not honor him as God or give thanks to him... (1:21a)

Indeed, Paul writes that they "knew God." They had a direct, unmediated, face-to-face relationship with their Maker in the Garden. As their Creator, God was the only one deserving of their loyalty and worship. And yet, in spite of their knowledge and their obvious dependence on God for their first breath and every one thereafter, "they did not honor God as God, or give thanks."

The serpent's deceptive assertion to Eve was that in eating the fruit "you will be like God" (Gen 3:5). That was of course a lie (for God as Creator is unique in his glory, so that no one is or can be like him); and it was just that misconception that the serpent's master, Satan, had himself succumbed to (see Isa 14:14, where at the root of Lucifer's rebellion is seen the prideful claim that "I will make myself like the Most High").

Adam and Eve did not honor God "as God"; that is, they did not acknowledge and submit to his unique glory. In taking steps they thought would lead them to "be like him," they were rejecting that uniqueness and refusing to take a dependent posture of gratitude ("give thanks") before their Maker.

Having denied the foundation of true worship (the unique glory of God), Adam and Eve inevitably plunged into false worship. That is exactly what we see in the ensuing verses (1:21b–25):

- "they became futile in their thinking" (21)
- "their foolish hearts were darkened" (21)
- "they became fools" (22)

- "they exchanged the glory of the immortal God for images" (23)
- "they exchanged the truth of God for a lie" (25)
- they "worshipped and served the creature rather than the Creator" (25)

Thus we see that *worship was the central issue in the fall.* The crucial question before Adam and Eve, and indeed before every human being in history, is: "*Whom are you going to worship?* Who is going to be on the throne of your life?"

Adam and Eve answered the question wrongly, and they carried the entire race with them into mutiny against their Creator. Jesus, on the other hand, would answer the same question correctly, right in Satan's face (Matt 4:10): "You will worship the Lord your God and serve him *only.*" And it would take the sacrifice of God's own Son to buy back his rebellious children.

Tozer highlights the centrality of worship to the entire New Testament account:

> Why did Christ come? Why was he conceived? Why was he born? Why was he crucified? Why did he rise again? Why is he now at the right hand of the Father? The answer to all these questions is in order *that he might make worshipers out of rebels*; in order that he might restore us again to the place of worship we knew when we were first created.[2]

Jesus through his redeeming work has made it possible for us to become the worshipers we were created to be, instead of the rebels we had become.

Paul will go on in Romans to expound the mighty work by which God would make this happen.

(For a fuller, more academic exposition, see Ronald E. Man, "False and True Worship in Romans 1.")

[*Worship Notes* 8.9, September 2013]

---

2. Tozer, *Worship: The Missing Jewel*, 19. Emphasis added.

5

"To him be the glory forever"
Paul's Doxology in Romans 11:33–36

THEOLOGY

Paul's explanation in Romans of the ramifications of the fall (1:18–32) and the ensuing blackness of sin that has engulfed the human race (3:9–18, 23) makes the gospel shine all the more brightly as he expounds on it in the ensuing chapters.

He shows how the gospel is indeed "the power of God for salvation to everyone who believes" (1:16), for through it God has showered upon believers:

- the righteousness of God through faith in Jesus Christ (3:22; 5:19)
- justification by his grace as a gift (3:24, 26; 4:5; 5:1)
- redemption (3:24)
- propitiation (3:25)
- peace with God (5:1)
- grace (5:2; 5:15)
- reconciliation (5:11)
- salvation as a free gift (5:17; 6:23)
- life (5:18)

- eternal life (5:21)
- newness of life (6:4)
- resurrection life (6:5)
- deliverance from condemnation (8:1)
- life in the Spirit (8:1–11)
- adoption (8:15)
- mercy (11:30)

Paul then expounds in chapters 9–11 on the mystery of God's purposes for Israel and the Gentiles, and how his grace, mercy, and sovereignty infuse these purposes.

DOXOLOGY

After this profound theological treatise in chapters 1–11 on the gospel and God's work in the world (and before turning to practical applications in chapters 12–16), Paul bursts forth in praise to the wise and utterly sovereign God whose ways he has been privileged to plumb so profoundly:

> Oh, the depth of the riches and wisdom and knowledge of God!
> How unsearchable are his judgments and how inscrutable his ways!
> "For who has known the mind of the Lord,
> or who has been his counselor?
> Or who has given a gift to him that he might be repaid?"
> For from him and through him and to him are all things.
> To him be glory forever! Amen. (11:33–36)

Paul turns from *theology* to *doxology*, and shows us the intimate and necessary connection between the two. As the late John Stott eloquently put it:

> It is important to note from Romans 1–11 that theology (our belief about God) and doxology (our worship of God) should never be separated.
> On the one hand, there can be *no doxology without theology*. It is not possible to worship an unknown god. All true worship is a response to the self-revelation of God in Christ and Scripture, and arises from our reflection on who he is and what he has done. It was the tremendous truths of Romans 1–11 which provoked Paul's outburst of praise in verses 33–36 of chapter 11. The worship of

God is evoked, informed and inspired by the vision of God. Worship without theology is bound to degenerate into idolatry. Hence the indispensable place of Scripture in both public and private devotion. It is the Word of God which calls forth the worship of God.

On the other hand, there should be *no theology without doxology*. There is something fundamentally flawed about a purely academic interest in God. God is not an appropriate object for cool, critical, detached, scientific observation and evaluation. No, the true knowledge of God will always lead us to worship, as it did Paul. Our place is on our faces before him in adoration.

As I believe Bishop Handley Moule said at the end of the last century, we must "beware equally of an undevotional theology and of an untheological devotion.[1]

Geoffrey Wainwright agrees:

> The ascription of praise with which a Chrysostom, an Augustine, or a Calvin ended their sermons was no mere formality: It indicated the intention of the sermon itself and its aim of bringing others also to the praise of God on account of what had been proclaimed in Scripture and sermon.[2]

And elsewhere Wainwright points out:

> The second-order activity of theology is therefore, at its own level, properly doxological: the theologian is truly theologian when, in his very theologizing, he is listening for the "echo of a voice" and is contributing, even if indirectly, to the human praise of God.[3]

But of course there is nothing "indirect" about Paul's approach! His full-throated response finds resonance with Isaac Watts' trinitarian hymn "We Give Immortal Praise," which ends like this:

> Almighty God, to Thee
> Be endless honours done,
> The undivided Three,
> And the mysterious One.
> Where reason fails, with all her powers,
> There faith prevails, and love adores.

---

1. Stott, *Romans*, 311–12.)
2. Wainwright, " Praise of God," 38.
3. Wainwright, *Doxology*, 2.

After the most profound theological exposition ever written, Paul necessarily comes to the end of himself, and his reason falters before the vastness of God's glory: there he bows the knee in faith and love, and breathlessly exclaims that

> from him and
> through him and
> to him
> are all things.
> To him be glory forever! Amen.

[*Worship Notes* 16.8, September 2021]

6

Yes and Amen
God's Program in Two Words
(2 Corinthians 1:20)

THE GOSPEL IN MINIATURE

Nestled in the opening strains of Paul's Second Epistle to the Corinthians is a statement which plumbs the depths of God's redemptive work through Christ and the relationship with him which we enjoy because of it.

THE CONTEXT

The context finds Paul addressing the charge of insincerity to which he found himself vulnerable in Corinth because of a change in his plans for revisiting that city. He had to redirect his itinerary, and now he wants to make it clear to the Corinthian believers that he is not one to vacillate: he is a man of his word (1:17). The reason Paul finds this so important to emphasize is that he wants them to understand that there is no mixed message and no unclear sound from the trumpet when it comes to the gospel he proclaimed to them. "As God is faithful, our word to you is not yes and no" (1:18). There is unequivocally one way of salvation, and this is the message which Paul and his companions (Silvanus and Timothy, 1:19) preached to the Corinthians—without wavering, without apology, without compromise, without vacillation (1:18–19). They were faithful communicators of God's plan of salvation.

YES

The faithfulness of the messengers is but a dim reflection of the way God himself has dealt with the Corinthians:

> For all the promises of God find their Yes in him [Christ]. (1:20a)

God has faithfully fulfilled all his promises in his Son; in Jesus Christ all these promises receive a resounding "Yes!":

1. All the promises inherent in God's creation of the world for humanity to rule over, and in God's creation of man in his image, for fellowship with himself.

2. All the promises extended to fallen humanity concerning redemption to come, from Genesis 3:16 to the sacrificial system of Israel to the Messianic and redemptive prophecies of the Old Testament:

   - the promise to Eve concerning her seed (Gen 3:16),
   - to Abraham concerning his seed and the blessing of the world (Gen 12:1–3; 22:15–18),
   - to Moses concerning the prophet like himself (Deut 18:18),
   - to David concerning his Son who would sit on his throne forever (1 Sam 7:12–13),
   - to Isaiah concerning a virgin-born Child (7:14) and eternal King (9:2, 6–7), and a Suffering Servant whose travails would satisfy God (52:13—53:12).

3. All of these find their fulfillment in Christ, along with a host of other hints and foreshadowings and types and hopes (cf. Luke 24:25–27; Acts 2:16–36; 3:22–25; 7:2–53; Rom 1:2–3, 16–17; 3:21–26; 1 Cor 5:7–8; 10:1–4; Eph 2:13–14; Heb 1:1–2; 3:5–6; 4:8–9; 7:17–22, 26–28; 8:5; 9:8–15, 24–26; 10:1–18; 11:39–40; 12:18–24; 13:9–10, 11–12, 14; 1 Pet 1:10–12).

All of these promises (and many others) find their Yes, their fulfillment, "in him." Jesus himself is the message (cf. 1:19, "the Son of God, Christ Jesus, who was preached among you by us"): he is the personification of God's stupendous plan for mankind; he is the grand and glorious exclamation point to all that God has revealed about himself; he is the "Yes!" to all that God in his grace has intended for us.

AMEN

God has planned it all and brought it to fruition through the saving work of his Son; it is left for us simply to respond and receive and adore:

> That is why it is through him [Christ] that we utter our Amen to
> God for his glory. (1:20b)

"That is why" emphasizes that our part is completely and utterly dependent on God's part: he has initiated and consummated his saving purposes on our behalf. Our response is "through him [Christ]," in acknowledgment of God's *Yes* to us through the redemptive work of Jesus; and that response is summarized by Paul as "our *Amen*." Paul is using a figure of speech (known as synecdoche) where a small part is used to represent a much larger whole; by it Paul indicates that all of our responses of prayer and praise and worship, which are so often punctuated with a final "Amen" (meaning "it is true" or "so be it"), are expressions of grateful assent and surrender to God's loving purposes for us in Christ.

More than that, our entire lives (which is the true New Testament scope and realm of worship, according to John 4:23 and Romans 12:1) are to be a confirmation and reflection of the wondrous work God has wrought in us. Our "Amen" is the full-orbed response of love, with all of our heart, soul, mind and strength (Mark 12:30), to God's "Yes" to us in Jesus; and this love we express through life- and lifestyle-pervading worship.

ALL OF CHRIST

It should be noticed that Jesus Christ is not only the message (1:19); not only is he the fulfillment of the many promises of God (1:20a); not only is he the subject and object of our adoring and grateful response of "Amen" (1:20b): Jesus Christ is *the active agent* in our response of worship to God for all that he done for us in His Son. Our Amen is not just to him, or for him—our Amen of response is actually "through him" (1:20b). Jesus does not leave us in our (albeit redeemed) frailty and weakness to drum up an appropriate response to God for his magnificent promises and their coming to fruition in his Son; no, Jesus leads the way as our Mediator in returning to the Father praise and honor and thanks for his redeeming work, for "summing all things up in Christ" (Eph 1:10).

And so our own response is but an echo of our High Priest's, and it gives our Maker pleasure—not because we have brought a level or quality or quantity of response appropriate to or worthy of his glory; but because the living Christ himself has made our response for us, and in so doing has made it perfect and worthy and acceptable. That perfect worship which God must and does require is effected by our Substitute and is credited to our account; in so doing God is indeed "working in us that which is pleasing in his sight" (Heb 13:21), with the result that "no man may boast" (1 Cor 1:29).

Our *Amen* (initiated and carried out through Christ) completes and complements God's *Yes* to us in Christ; so it is in Christ that the entire duality is carried out and completed: he is the operative force both in the God-to-man movement of *Yes*, and in the man-to-God response of *Amen*. Thus in Christ we see the fulfillment of the foundational Revelation/Response paradigm of Scripture (see part 2, chapter 1): he is the agent of God's Revelation ("Yes") and also the agent of our Response back to God ("Amen"). Thus 2 Corinthians 1:20 brilliantly expresses in microcosm the centrality of Christ and his work, in much the same way as does Hebrews 2:12 (see part 5, chapter 2).

TO THE GLORY OF GOD

God's plan, its fulfillment in Christ, and the response of worship on our part: all these aspects work together to evoke the "praise of his glory" (Eph 1:6, 12, 14) through God's sovereign and gracious "Yes" to us in Jesus Christ, and through our humble and never-ending response of "Amen."

God has said, "Here is my Son, offered up for your salvation. Yes!"

We reply, "Thank you, Father. Thank you, Jesus. Amen!"

And thus God thus brings great glory to his blessed name!

[*Worship Notes* 9.2, February 2014)

7

Worship in the Book of Hebrews

Hebrews is a whole world of its own when it comes to New Testament teachings about worship. Here are some testimonies to its greatness and uniqueness:

> Hebrews presents the most complete and fully integrated theology of worship in the New Testament. All the important categories of Old Testament thinking on this subject—sanctuary, sacrifice, altar, priesthood and covenant—are taken up and related to the person and work of Jesus Christ. More than any other New Testament document, Hebrews makes it clear that the inauguration of the new covenant by Jesus means the fulfillment and replacement of the whole pattern of approach to God established under the Mosaic covenant. The writer proclaims the end of that earthly cult, by expounding Christ's work as the ultimate, heavenly cult.
>
> In short, then, if we take Christ out of Hebrews, we are left with nothing. He is the substance of the book and without him the whole reality of the new covenant and the life of Christian belief and worship collapses. The writer, then, does not spare his readers the glory of Christ's person and work nor the demands this places upon them. There is no "laid back religion" in Hebrews. The author expects his addressees to attend to what is being said with diligence and urgency. The change of worship brought about through Christ is irreversible, and its consequences are inevitably pressing.[1]

---

1. Due, *Created for Worship*, 156.

The fact that Jesus Christ is the leader of our worship, the high priest who forgives us our sins and leads us into the holy presence of the Father, is the central theme of the epistle to the Hebrews.[2]

There is, indeed, no book in Holy Scripture which speaks so clearly of the priesthood of Christ, which so highly exalts the virtue and dignity of that only true sacrifice which He offered by His death, which so abundantly deals with the issue of ceremonies as well as their abrogation, and, in a word, so fully explains that Christ is the end of the Law. Let us therefore not allow the Church of God or ourselves to be deprived of so great a benefit, but firmly defend the possession of it.[3]

A BETTER WAY

It is commonly held that the Letter to the Hebrews was written to Jewish Christians who because of persecution or the threat of it were in danger of returning to Judaism. The writer gives a resounding defense of the superiority of Christ and of the New Covenant he instituted, with the clearly implied question: "Why would you give all of this up for a superseded system which was just a shadow of the reality that has now come?"

Here is a list of all the things of which the writer says a better counterpart now exists under Christ:

A BETTER:

1:2–14	spokesman for God (the Son)
2:2–3	message (salvation)
3:3	rest
4:15	High Priest (tempted but sinless)
7:7, 15–17	priestly order (of Melchizedek)
7:21	priesthood (made with oath)
7:22	covenant (better guarantor)
7:27; 9:26	sacrifice (priest himself)
7:28	priest (perfect)
8:2; 9:11	Tabernacle
8:6	ministry (better covenant)

---

2. James Torrance, *Worship, Community and the Triune God of Grace*, 57.
3. Calvin, *Commentaries on Hebrews*.

8:6	covenant (based on better promises)
8:6	promises
8:11	knowledge of the Lord
9:12; 12:24	blood
9:12	redemption (eternal)
9:14; 10:22	cleansing (of conscience)
9:14–15	inheritance (eternal)
9:23	sacrifices
9:24	holy place (in heaven)
9:26; 10:12,14	frequency (once for all)
8:10; 10:16	law (written on heart, mind)
8:19	access (to holy place)
12:22	mountain/city (Zion)
12:28	kingdom (cannot be shaken)
13:9	food (grace)
13:10	altar (Christ)

A BETTER MEDIATOR

Above all, of course, the writer stunningly portrays the person of Christ as a vastly superior Mediator and Priest than was offered by the Old Covenant. And he is powerfully portrayed in both his deity and his humanity, as seen especially in chapters 1 and 2.

Two Natures and Roles (1–2)

Worship of *the Son*

- His deity (1:1–4)
- His authority (1:5–14)

As God's ultimate spokesman and representative (1:1–3,5), Christ is seen to be superior to the angels (1:4–7) and indeed deserving of worship himself (1:6).

Worship by *the Son*

- His humanity (2:6–11)
- His priesthood (2:12–18; also 4:14–16)

As one of us, the incarnate Son exercises a priestly ministry on our behalf as our Substitute (2:9, 14–15, 17) and indeed (post-ascension) as the Mediator of our praise: he is our great Worship Leader (2:12b).

Summary (3:1): Apostle and High Priest

Here the writer summarizes Christ's dual, bidirectional role: first as Apostle, as the Mediator of between God and man and the conduit of God's message to man (2:12a); and also as Priest, as the Mediator between man and God and the conduit of man's response back to God (2:12b).

Two Priesthoods (5–10)

Contrasting the Two Priesthoods

The author extensively develops the theme of Christ's priesthood and its distinctive differences from the Levitical priesthood under the Old Covenant.

Levitical Priesthood/Order of Aaron	Priesthood of Christ/Order of Melchizedek
Descended from Levi, Aaron (7:5, 11)	Descended from Judah (7:14)
Sinful (5:3; 7:27)	"holy, innocent, unstained, separated from sinners" (7:26)
Weak (5:2; 7:28)	Perfect (5:9; 7:28; 10:14)
Many, because mortal/temporary (7:2)	One, permanent priesthood (lives forever) (7:24)
Could only purify the flesh (9:13)	Can purify the conscience (9:14)
Had to offer for own sins (5:3; 7:27; 9:7)	Sinless (7:26)
Had to offer same sacrifices repeatedly (5:1; 7:27; 9:25; 10:1, 3, 11)	One sacrifice (7:27; 9:12, 26, 28; 10:10, 12, 14)
Offered blood of animals (9:18–22; 10:4)	Offered himself, own blood (7:27; 9:12, 25–26); "better sacrifices" (9:23)
Offerings could not make perfect or perfect the conscience (5:9; 7:11, 18; 9:9; 10:1)	Can purify conscience (9:14), perfect those sanctified (10:14)
Served shadow tent/tabernacle (8:5; 9:23–24)	Serves true tabernacle (8:2; 9:11, 23–24)
Could not take away sins (10:11)	Redeems from sins committed under Old Covenant (9:15); grants eternal redemption (9:12); saves forever (7:25)
Served an imperfect covenant (8:7)	"guarantor of a better covenant" (7:22; 8:6)
Inferior ministry based on inferior promises (8:6)	Better ministry based on better promises (8:6)

Christ like Melchizedek (Gen 14:18–20; Ps 110:4; Heb 5–7)

1. "king of Salem" (7:1); "king of righteousness" (7:2); without human pedigree (7:3, 6); greater than Abraham and Levi (7:6–10); not from priestly line (7:11–16; 8:4) (so too Christ)

2. Gen 14:18–20: Melchizedek as mediator; notice the bidirectional nature of Melchizedek's actions (we will see Christ's bidirectional mediation as well in part 5, chapter 2):

   - he blesses Abraham on behalf of God, and
   - blesses God on behalf of Abraham:

   And [Melchizedek] blessed him and said,
      "Blessed be Abram by God Most High,

> Possessor of heaven and earth;
> and blessed be God Most High,
> who has delivered your enemies into your hand!"

Entering the heavenly tabernacle (his sacrifice) (9:11–14, 24; 10:5–9)

> [Jesus] entered once for all into the holy places, not by means of the blood of goats and calves but by means of his own blood, thus securing an eternal redemption. (Heb 9:12)

Ministering in the heavenly tabernacle (his session and ongoing ministry) (8:1–2)

> We have such a high priest, one who is seated at the right hand of the throne of the Majesty in heaven, a minister in the holy places, in the true tent that the Lord set up, not man. (Heb 8:1–2)

Summary (10:11–14)

> And every priest stands daily at his service, offering repeatedly the same sacrifices, which can never take away sins. But when Christ had offered for all time a single sacrifice for sins, he sat down at the right hand of God, waiting from that time until his enemies should be made a footstool for his feet. For by a single offering he has perfected for all time those who are being sanctified.

A BETTER WORSHIP (10:19–22)

> Therefore, brethren, since we have confidence to enter the holy places by the blood of Jesus, by the new and living way that he opened for us through the curtain, that is, through his flesh, and since we have a great priest over the house of God, let us draw near with a true heart in full assurance of faith, with our hearts sprinkled clean from an evil conscience and our bodies washed with pure water.

The author climatically makes application in these verses: in light of all the ways in which Christ and the New Covenant have been shown to be infinitely superior to the old system ("Therefore," 10:19), the logical response is to "draw near in full assurance of faith" (10:22). The Greek word translated "draw near" is used several times in the book (4:16; 7:25; 10:1,22; 11:6; 12:18, 22; see also 1 Pet 2:4–5). It was a common Old Testament word for the approach of worship by the priests; but now of course it has a deeper and richer significance, as the approach is to God in heaven, and by all believers.

Full access has been obtained through the past work of Christ (10:19b–20) as well as his *present* work (10:21: "since we *have* a great priest over the house of God"). Thus the writer highlights these two emphases of Christ's past *and* present work as the ground of our confident and sure (10:19–22) access to the presence of the Father: not only has Christ opened and shown us the way; but *he takes us with him*. "The invitation of the book of Hebrews is to go where he goes."[4]

Both the past and present aspects of Christ's work are quite prominent through the book (though his present work, even though so crucial, is often overlooked):

PAST	PRESENT
1:3	
2:9–10	
	2:12
2:14–17	
	2:18
	3:1
3:11	
4:14–17	
	4:18
5:7–8	
	7:25
7:26–27	
	8:1–2
	8:6
9:11–14	
9:23	

4. Cocksworth, *Holy, Holy, Holy*, 157.

	9:24
9:26	
10:10	
10:12–14	
10:19–20	
	10:21
12:2	
12:24	
13:12	
	13:15
13:20	
	13:21

And the fitting responses to all that the person and work of Christ have made available to us are indicated by the writer to be:

- confidence and assurance (10:22; 4:16)
- gratitude, reverence, awe (12:28)
- praise (13:15)

CONCLUSION: "THROUGH HIM" (13:15; 7:25; 2 COR 1:20; EPH 2:18; COL 3:17)

At the end of the epistle the writer emphasizes once more that our response to God is always mediated by Christ, the all-sufficient Priest, Mediator, and Leader of our worship:

> *Through him*, then, let us continually offer up a sacrifice of praise to God, that is, the fruit of lips that acknowledge his name." (13:15)

[*Worship Notes* 4.9, April 2009]

PART 5

Jesus and Our Worship

1

Jesus on Worship (John 4)

OLD COVENANT BARRIERS

The Old Covenant system of worship, in spite of its gracious provisions for relating to the covenant-keeping God of Israel (through a temporary covering of sin in anticipation of Christ's atoning work, Rom 3:24–25), nevertheless was a system that demonstrated strongly the distance that sin had put between God and even his own chosen people. Access to the presence of God (represented in the architecture of the Tabernacle) was severely proscribed. Entry into the Holy of Holies was reserved for the high priest alone, who himself could enter only once a year, on the Day of Atonement (see Leviticus 16).

The book of Hebrews clearly demonstrates how all the barriers of this Old Covenant system were destroyed, and the way into the presence of God made fully available, by the redeeming death of Christ on the cross. Hebrews 10:19–22 climactically encourages us to take full advantage of that free and unfettered access with confidence and assurance.

Jesus Christ came to remove other barriers as well: to break down the dividing wall between Jew and Gentile (Eph 2:14–20), male and female, slave and free (Gal 3:28). And in John 4 we see his barrier-breaking ways in full force.

PART 5. JESUS AND OUR WORSHIP

JESUS BREAKS DOWN GEOGRAPHICAL BARRIERS (4:3-4)

The Jews had a deep-seated contempt for the Samaritans, for a number of reasons: they were the product of Jewish and Gentile intermarriage; they rejected all but the first five books of the Old Testament; and they had instituted their own place and form of worship on Mount Gerizim. Jews in Jesus' day would show their animosity by going out of their way to avoid going through Samaria when traveling between Judea in the south and Galilee in the north (Samaria was situated between the two): they would cross over the Jordan River and go up the east side so as not to step on Samaritan soil.

Given this common practice among the Jews, it is particularly striking when we read at the beginning of John 4 that, in journeying from Judea to Galilee, Jesus "*had to* pass through Samaria" (4:4). This necessity was not a physical one, as other Jews demonstrated regularly by taking the trans-Jordan route. Rather it was *a divine necessity*; as we learn later in the chapter, Jesus had a divine appointment to keep in Samaria, and work to do for his Father there (4:32-34). And so he shuns precedent and breaches this geographical barrier by heading directly into "enemy territory."

JESUS BREAKS DOWN ETHNIC AND SOCIAL BARRIERS (4:5-9)

Having forged his own path right through this traditional geographical barrier, Jesus does another surprising thing. He strikes up a conversation with a Samaritan, and a woman at that (surprising the woman herself, 4:9; as well as the disciples, 4:27). Jesus readily dispenses with traditional taboos when there is a needy soul at stake.

JESUS BREAKS DOWN SPIRITUAL BARRIERS (4:10-15)

Jesus deepens his unconventional approach by offering this unlikely subject, representative of a despised race, the gift of eternal life, which he characterizes as living water. While she does not at first understand (thinking rather of physical water, such as she has come to draw), Jesus persists in explaining in explaining the unique nature of this water and its cure for spiritual thirst.

JESUS ON WORSHIP (JOHN 4)

JESUS BREAKS DOWN RELIGIOUS BARRIERS (4:16–26)

In response to Jesus' thorough (yet uncondemning) knowledge of her personal history, the woman raises the issue (whether it's in an attempt to change the subject, or out of genuine interest, we're not told) of the religious barrier that most sharply divided the Jews and the Samaritans: the location and nature of their respective systems of worship. And Jesus explodes the now-false dichotomy by explaining that he's changing the rules: under the age inaugurated by his coming, the question of "in this mountain" or "in Jerusalem" (in the Temple on Mount Moriah) isn't even the right question or sphere of inquiry anymore (4:21): rather, true worship, Jesus proclaims, must now be defined by being both "in spirit" and "[in] truth" (4:23). The issue is no longer *where* or *when* one worships, but *how*.

THE WORSHIP GOD SEEKS

Worship in spirit

Worship "in spirit" indicates that it must come from the inside out, from spirit—the internal, immaterial party of one's nature. (That this, rather than the Holy Spirit, is in view seems more likely because Jesus points out that "God is spirit" [4:24] as the reason why he must be approached in this way.) Worship must be from the heart, be sincere and genuine. Contained in this assertion is probably implied a contrast to the Jews, and especially their leaders, whom Jesus often castigated for practicing an external form of religion without an internal reality as its basis (see Matt 6:1–18; 23:23–28; etc).

Worship in truth

Worship must also be "in truth": it must be according to God's self-revelation and his revealed will. We must worship God as he really is, and as he wants to be worshiped (and ultimately, of course, this means it must be through Christ, 4:26, who is the Truth, John 14:6). This is in marked contrast to the Samaritans' worship, as Jesus makes clear to the woman: "You worship what you do not know" (4:22); by rejecting most of the Old Testament they had thereby rejected the true God.

Worship in spirit *and* truth

In our own day we see the same imbalances in one direction or the other as was true of the Jews and the Samaritans. There are plenty of highly religious people in our world who are very, very sincere about their beliefs and their worship; and they strive, through prayers and fasts and pilgrimages and even suicide bombings, to achieve favor and status with God. But of course, they are sincerely wrong: their worship is not according to truth. Likewise, we all know people who practice a "form of godliness" (2 Tim 3:5)—attending church, reciting the Apostles' Creed, taking the Lord's Supper, etc.—but without any apparent heart faith or true commitment to the Lord (though of course only God can judge their hearts).

Jesus says that worship must be *both* in spirit *and* in truth.

GOD SEEKS WORSHIPERS

One other crucial perspective on worship from Jesus' lips is found in 4:23: the Father is seeking worshipers. The Bible never says that God is seeking pastors, or missionaries, or Sunday School teachers, or Christian businessmen and -women. These are all worthy pursuits, but they are not what God wants first and foremost from us. Most of all, he wants us to be *worshipers*. We must fulfill the first and greatest commandment (to love God with our heart, soul, mind and strength—which is worship), before we turn to serve our neighbor, as the second greatest commandment commands. We must "be something" before God before we "do" something for him.

[*Worship Notes* 3.9, September 2008]

2

Jesus, Our True Worship Leader
"What God requires, he provides."

HOW GOD WORKS

In Galatians 3:3, Paul poses to his readers a rhetorical question:

> Are you so foolish? Having begun by the Spirit, are you now being perfected by the flesh?

To Paul the obvious answer is: having begun by the Spirit (through "hearing with faith," Gal 3:2), *of course* you're not now perfected by the flesh! In fact, Paul declares that it would be "foolish" for the Galatians to think so. Having begun by the Spirit, the continuing work of being perfected will be undergirded by the Spirit as well; later in the same epistle, Paul writes: "If we live by the Spirit, let us also keep in step with the Spirit" (5:25).

Paul is highlighting an important principle of the Christian faith: God commits himself to complete the good work he has begun in us (Phil 1:6). The Holy Spirit comes alongside to work in us and with us in the process of living the Christian life.

This is a crucial distinctive of New Testament Christianity, one which is borne out by a number of different passages, for example:

> Likewise the Spirit helps us in our weakness. For we do not know what to pray for as we ought, but the Spirit himself intercedes for us with groanings too deep for words. (Rom 8:26)

PART 5. JESUS AND OUR WORSHIP

We don't even know how to pray, but the Spirit will come alongside and help us.

> Therefore, my beloved, as you have always obeyed, so now, not only as in my presence but much more in my absence, work out your own salvation with fear and trembling, for it is God who works in you, both to will and to work for his good pleasure. (Phil 2:12–13)

We work out our salvation, but God is working in us, too.

> For this I toil, struggling with all his energy that he powerfully works within me. (Col 1:29)

Paul toils and struggles, but God provides strength.

> For the grace of God has appeared, bringing salvation for all people, training us to renounce ungodliness and worldly passions, and to live self-controlled, upright, and godly lives in the present age. (Titus 2:11–12)

The grace of God trains us for growth.

> But by the grace of God I am what I am, and his grace toward me was not in vain. On the contrary, I worked harder than any of them, though it was not I, but the grace of God that is with me. (1 Cor 15:10)

Paul worked harder than all, yet not alone: the grace of God enabled him.

> Test everything; hold fast what is good. Abstain from every form of evil. Now may the God of peace himself sanctify you completely, and may your whole spirit and soul and body be kept blameless at the coming of our Lord Jesus Christ. He who calls you is faithful; he will surely do it. (1 Thess 5:21–24)

We are to live holy lives, yet God is the One upon whom we can depend to sanctify us.

> Now may the God of peace who brought again from the dead our Lord Jesus, the great shepherd of the sheep, by the blood of the eternal covenant, equip you with every-thing good that you may do his will, working in us that which is pleasing in his sight, through Jesus Christ, to whom be glory forever and ever. Amen. (Heb 13:20–21)

We are to do God's will, yet the writer prays that he will equip us to do so; we are to live in a manner pleasing to the Lord, yet he will work that in us.

The purpose in piling up so many passages is to demonstrate the prevalence of this New Testament theme of *grace*: God doing for us what we cannot do for ourselves; or, in the words of Augustine, "What God requires, he provides."

God requires *perfect holiness* in order to enter heaven; we do not have that in ourselves, but in his grace Christ has provided that holiness for us. That is *God's grace for our salvation*. God also wants us to live *a holy life* on earth (1 Pet 1:15–16); we certainly can't do that ourselves, but, as we have just seen, God has promised to help those who are in Christ in that quest. That is *God's grace for our sanctification*.

God also deserves, and demands, *perfect worship*. What we want to examine here is God's wonderful provision for us in that arena as well: we want to consider *God's grace for our worship*. What God requires of our worship, he provides for us *in Jesus Christ*.

GOD'S GRACE FOR OUR WORSHIP

Jesus, Our High Priest

Jesus' high priestly ministry was not completed when he offered himself as the once-for-all and once-for-all-time sacrifice for sin. A major emphasis of the book of Hebrews is the *continuing* ministry of our living High Priest. (See part 4, chapter 7). The writer makes clear that "we *have* [not *had*] a great high priest" in Jesus Christ:

The writer also makes clear that Jesus (unlike the priests of old) holds his priestly office forever:

> As he says also in another place, "You are a priest forever, after the order of Melchizedek." (5:6, quoting Ps 110:4)

> Jesus has gone as a forerunner on our behalf, having become a high priest forever after the order of Melchizedek. (6:20)

> For it is witnessed of him, "You are a priest forever, after the order of Melchizedek." (7:17)

> But this one was made a priest with an oath by the one who said to him: "The Lord has sworn and will not change his mind, 'You are a priest forever.'" (7:21)

> The former priests were many in number because they were prevented by death from continuing in office, but he holds his priesthood permanently, because he continues forever. Consequently, he is able to save to the uttermost those who draw near to God through him, since he always lives to make intercession for them. (7:23–25)

Consequently, the writer, in his climactic "therefore" verses of application in chapter 10, cites *two* reasons we can draw near to God in worship:

> Therefore, brothers, since we have confidence to enter the holy places by the blood of Jesus, by the new and living way that he opened for us through the curtain, that is, through his flesh, [Reason 1: because of the *past* work of Christ] and since we have a great priest over the house of God, [Reason 2: because of the *present*, priestly work of Christ] let us draw near with a true heart in full assurance of faith, with our hearts sprinkled clean from an evil conscience and our bodies washed with pure water. (10:19–22)

Jesus, Our Mediator

One Mediator

Similarly, Paul states in no uncertain terms that "there is one God, and one Mediator between man and God, the man Christ Jesus" (1 Tim 2:5). Not that Jesus *was*, but *is* the "one Mediator between man and God." As our living High Priest, and as still a man, he continues to mediate between humanity and God.

This is important historically, as well as theologically, because of what has been pointed out about the increasing neglect during the Middle Ages of Christ's continuing humanity. Geoffrey Wainwright cites Josef Jungmann in this regard:

> Jungmann . . . showed how anti-Arian motives eventually came to shift the emphasis from the human Christ, or the incarnate Son in His continuing mediatorial function, to the Son as the Second Person of the Trinity and therefore himself a recipient of worship. . . . Jungmann proved conclusively from later liturgies that the liturgical result of the Arian controversy in both East and West was that stress was now placed not on what unites us to God (Christ as one

of us in His human nature, Christ as our brother), but on what separates us from God (God's infinite majesty).[1]

In other words, the crucial defense of Christ's deity, in the face of dangerous heresies calling it into question, eventually led to a downplaying of Christ's full and complete (and continuing) humanity. Hence, the church began to develop the idea that access to God was possible only through human agencies, such as a priest, the Virgin Mary, or one of the saints. Thomas Torrance puts it this way:

> When the Humanity of Christ is depreciated or whenever it is obscured by the sheer majesty of his Deity then the need for some other human mediation creeps in—hence in the Dark and Middle Ages arose the need for a human priesthood to mediate between sinful humanity and the exalted Christ, the majestic Judge and King.[2]

One of the major rallying cries of the Reformation (especially of Calvin) was restoring the concept of the sole priesthood and mediatorship of Christ, without the need for intermediating agents like priests, saints, or Mary. Again Thomas Torrance:

> At the Reformation this doctrine [justification by Christ] had immediate effect in the overthrow of Roman sacerdotalism—Jesus Christ is our sole Priest. He is the one and only Man who can mediate between us and God, so that we approach God solely through the mediation of the Humanity of Jesus, through His incarnate Priesthood.... There was of course no denial of the Deity of Christ by the Reformers—on the contrary they restored the purity of faith in Christ as God through overthrowing the accretions that compromised it; but they also restored the place occupied in the New Testament and the Early Church by the Humanity of Christ, as He who took our human nature in order to be our Priest, as He who takes our side and is our Advocate before the judgment of God, and who once and for all has wrought out atonement for us in His sacrifice on the Cross, and therefore as He who eternally stands in for us as our heavenly Mediator and High-Priest.[3]

---

1. Wainwright, *Doxology*, 63; citing Josef Jungmann, *Place of Christ in Liturgical Prayer*.
2. Thomas Torrance, *Theology in Reconstruction*, 167.
3. Thomas Torrance, *Theology in Reconstruction*, 166–67.

PART 5. JESUS AND OUR WORSHIP

Two-Way Mediation

In the Old Testament, one finds a double agency of mediation back and forth between God and man, which reflects the foundational biblical pattern of Revelation and Response (see part 2, chapter 1). God spoke to Moses on the mountain, and his job was to go down and faithfully communicate the Lord's revelation to the people of Israel; he was God's chosen mediator *from himself to man*. His brother Aaron (the first high priest) was to represent, through the sacrificial system, the people in their response of worship back to God; he was the appointed mediator *from man to God*.

Later in Israel's history one sees a similar pattern: the prophet was to serve as God's mouthpiece, communicating his revealed message to the people, as mediator *between God and man*. We read explicitly that "the word of the Lord came" to the prophets Samuel (1 Sam 15:10), Nathan (2 Sam 7:4; 1 Chron 17:3), Gad (2 Sam 24:11), Jehu (1 Kings 16:1, 7), Elijah (1 Kings 17:2, 8; 18:1; 19:9; 21:17; 21:28), Shemaiah (2 Chron 11:2; 12:7), Isaiah (2 Kings 20:4; Isa 38:4), Jeremiah (Jer 1:2, 4, 11, 13; 2:1; etc.), Ezekiel (Ezek 1:3; 3:16; etc.), Hosea (Hosea 1:1), Joel (Joel 1:1), Jonah (1:1; 3:1), Micah (Micah 1:1), Zephaniah (Zeph 1:1), and Zechariah (Zech 1:1,7). And the priests continued as mediators *between man and God*, representing the former in their worship response.

In the New Testament, we learn the wonderful truth that Jesus Christ now fills *both* of those mediatorial roles. As the unique God-man, he mediates both between God and man, *and* man and God.

Hebrews 1 focuses on the *deity* of Christ; as God he is worthy to *receive* worship ("Let all God's angels worship him," v. 6). His *humanity* is the focus of Hebrews 2 ("But we see him who for a little while was made lower than the angels, namely Jesus," v. 9a; "For he who sanctifies and those who are sanctified all have one source. That is why he is not ashamed to call them brethren," v. 11; "Since therefore the children share in flesh and blood, he himself likewise partook of the same things," v. 14a; "Therefore he had to be made like his brethren in every respect," v. 17a); he is therefore qualified to *give* worship as well ("In the midst of the congregation I will sing your praise," v. 12b).

This two-way mediation is beautifully and concisely portrayed in Hebrews 2:12 (as is also the climactic fulfillment of the Revelation-Response paradigm in him). Here the writer is quoting from Psalm 22 (which of course foretells the crucifixion of Christ, as he appropriates to himself the opening cry of verse 1 as he hangs on the cross: "My God, My God, why have you forsaken me?" Matt 27:46; Mark 15:34). Psalm 22:22, quoted in Hebrews 2:12, is the first verse of the second section of the Psalm, which looks beyond the suffering of the Messiah to the victory to follow. The writer of Hebrews amazingly states that *these are the words of Christ himself*, speaking to his Father:

> [Revelation: God to man]
> "I will tell of your name to my brethren;
>
> [Response: man to God]
> and in the midst of the congregation I will sing your praise."

Jesus, the Revealer of the Father

In the first half of Hebrews 2:12, Jesus speaks of his ministry of proclamation of God's name (that is, of his Person and nature), of mediating the revelation of God to man. This clearly was his role during his earthly sojourn:

> "No one knows the Son except the Father, and no one knows the Father except the Son and anyone to whom the Son wills to reveal him." (Matt 11:27b)

> No one has ever seen God; the only God, who is at the Father's side, he has made him known. (John 1:18)

But in Hebrews 2:12, Jesus (speaking post-cross, post-glorification) claims a *continuing* role in this regard. He hints at this as he prays to his Father in the upper room on the night before his crucifixion (looking beyond the cross and the resurrection):

> "I made known to them your name, and I will *continue* to make it known. (John 17:26a)

And in the opening statement of his second volume (the book of Acts), Luke hearkens back to his gospel account in this way:

> In the first book, O Theophilus, I have dealt with all that Jesus *began* to do and teach . . . (Acts 1:1)

Luke definitely seems to be implying that in Acts he will relate what Jesus *continues* "to do and to teach"—now through the Holy Spirit, the apostles, other human instruments, and through the church itself.

These passages, as well as Hebrews 2:12, show that the ministry of revealing the Father is *still Christ's ministry*. And so as we preach and teach the Word in any context, we need to be humbly and gratefully aware that we are representing Christ, whose ministry it still is to reveal the Father.

With this perspective in mind, Paul's familiar words in Colossians 3:16, "Let the word of Christ dwell in you richly," come alive in an astonishing way: rather than seeing "of Christ" as merely an *objective* genitive (the word *about* Christ), we may well see Paul intending it as a *subjective* genitive (that is, the word *that comes from* Christ himself). The meaning of this verse thus takes on a much deeper, active, and vibrant sense—and indeed we can begin to see just how "richly" that word may dwell among us!

Here are some testimonies demonstrating this understanding of the truth of Christ's continuing proclamation to his church in and through his servants:

> In Scripture reading and sermon, in sacrament and in liturgical action, Christ proclaims God to man.[4]

> The preacher is the servant of the Word. His sermon puts at Christ's disposal the living language of the present day, with its associations with the everyday life of the congregation. It permits Christ to preach His Word through the mouth of the contemporary Church, as he has already through the Apostolic Church,[5]

> When the Church is proclaiming the word of God, Christ is still proclaiming His gospel."[6]

Jesus, Our Worship Leader

Even more remarkable perhaps are the implications of the *second* half of Hebrews 2:12, where Jesus tells the Father: "in the midst of the congregation I will sing your praise." As our great High Priest, he represents us before the Father. He not only mediates our response of praise, he *participates* in it! This concept plumbs one of the most profound depths of the mystery of the

---

4. Nicholls, *Jacob's Ladder: The Meaning of Worship*, 38.
5. Nicholls, *Jacob's Ladder: The Meaning of Worship*, 42.
6. Crichton, "Theology of Worship," in Jones, *Study of Liturgy*, 28; quoting Second Vatican Council, *Constitution on the Liturgy* 7.33.

incarnation: that Jesus Christ, who as God deserves and receives worship (Heb 1:6), should also as man *be a worshiper himself*!

Calvin, in his commentary on Hebrews, explains that in 2:12 we see that "Christ is the chief Conductor of our hymns."[7] And the writer of Hebrews in 8:1 refers to Christ as a "*leitourgos* [liturgist] in the holy places."

That Christ leads the congregation in their praise is not explicitly stated in Hebrews 2:12, but is clearly implied in harmony with the rest of Hebrews and the New Testament. As already examined, his continuing priesthood is a major theme in Hebrews, and one crucial activity of a priest is *leading the people in worship*. It stands to reason that our Priest is the One who must lead us in offering our sacrifice, which is now identified as a "*sacrifice of praise*" (Heb 13:15), and this verse explicitly states that we make that sacrifice "*through him.*" It is a natural conclusion that our praises would be in conjunction with, motivated by, empowered by, and even led, by Christ's praises "in the midst of the assembly" (Heb 2:12b).

When Christ our model and brother praises the Father, he leads the way for us. Because we are in union with him, his worship is our worship. Through him we come into the Father's presence in worship; we come clothed in his righteousness, and he bears up our weak offerings of worship and makes them one with his own perfect offering of praise. James Torrance has aptly summarized Jesus' role: "The real agent in all true worship is Jesus Christ."[8] He is not an observer—he is the *Leader* of our worship. As Thomas Torrance explains:

> The Church on earth lives and acts only as it is directed by its heavenly Lord, and only in such a way that His Ministry is reflected in the midst of its ministry and worship. Therefore from first to last the worship and ministry of the Church on earth must be governed by the fact that Christ substitutes himself in our place, and that our humanity with its own acts of worship, is displaced by his, so that we appear before God not in our own name, not in our own significance, not in virtue of our own acts of confession, contrition, worship, and thanksgiving, but solely in the name of Christ and solely in virtue of what He has done in our name and on our behalf, and in our stead. Justification by Christ alone means that from first to last in the worship of God and in the ministry of the Gospel Christ himself is central, and that we draw near in worship and service only through letting Him take our place. He only is Priest. He only

---

7. John Calvin, *Commentaries on the Epistle to the Hebrews*, on 2:12.
8. James Torrance, *Worship, Community and the Triune God of Grace*, 17.

represents humanity. He only has an offering with which to appear before God and with which God is well-pleased. He only presents our prayers before God, and He only is our praise and thanksgiving and worship as we appear before the face of the Father. Nothing in our hands we bring—simply to His Cross we cling.[9]

Christ in Our Place

In its essence, New Testament worship centers in Jesus Christ and his two-way mediating ministry. Our worship is in, through, with, and by Jesus Christ.

> Accordingly, the Church's worship will be best conformed to its true nature when its pattern echoes the Christological pattern we have seen in Scripture. In the first place, the Church must be attentive to the proclamation of the Word. . . . The second aspect of Christian worship is our joining in the *latreia* of Christ, offering through Him the sacrifice of praise and thanksgiving to the Father, in the power of the Holy Spirit.[10]

> Without the work of Christ, bringing God down to men, and gathering men in Himself before God, there can be no worship at all, and indeed no Church.[11]

> Christ [is] the true though invisible Celebrant of all that is done.[12]

> Christ is the One in whom Word and response are united.[13]

SOME IMPLICATIONS AND CORRECTIVES FOR OUR WORSHIP

The nature of true worship

James Torrance warned against what he termed the quasi-"Unitarian" worship that characterizes much evangelical practice:

---

9. Thomas Torrance, *Theology in Reconstruction*, 167.
10. Nicholls, *Jacob's Ladder: The Meaning of Worship*, 27–28.
11. Nicholls, *Jacob's Ladder: The Meaning of Worship*, 36.
12. Nicholls, *Jacob's Ladder: The Meaning of Worship*, 39.
13. Nicholls, *Jacob's Ladder: The Meaning of Worship*, 40.

We sit in the pew watching the minister "doing his thing," exhorting us "to do our thing," until we go home thinking we have done our duty for another week! This kind of do-it-yourself-with-the-help-of-the-minister worship is what... the ancient church would have called Arian or Pelagian.[14]

True worship, Torrance insists, is richly trinitarian:

> There is only one true Priest through whom and with whom we draw near to God our Father. There is only one Mediator between God and humanity. There is only one offering which is truly acceptable to God, and it is not ours. It is the offering by which He has sanctified for all time those who come to God by Him (Heb 2:11; 10:10, 14). There is only one who can lead us into the presence of the Father by His sacrifice on the cross.[15]

Worship is thus, according to Torrance, "the gift of participating through the Spirit in the incarnate Son's communion with the Father."[16] Or as John Witvliet has put it:

> The Father receives our worship,
> The Son perfects our worship,
> The Holy Spirit prompts our worship.[17]

The paradigm of true worship

Christ himself is the fulfillment of the biblical pattern of Revelation and Response that underlies all true worship (Old and New Testament). We have seen that Christ himself leads both parts in his two-way mediation as the incarnate God-man. That gives *both* aspects a sublime and holy importance in the corporate gatherings of God's people: not just the revelation of God's truth (though that is primary), but also the response of the people, which Jesus himself sees as so important that he is in their midst leading it!

---

14. James Torrance, *Worship, Community and the Triune God of Grace*, 21.
15. James Torrance, *Worship, Community and the Triune God of Grace*, 21.
16. James Torrance, *Worship, Community and the Triune God of Grace*, 30.
17. Witvliet, unpublished lecture. See also his "The Trinitarian DNA of Christian Worship." On the Holy Spirit's role in worship, see part 1, chapter 2: "Spirit-Enabled Worship."

PART 5. JESUS AND OUR WORSHIP

The power of true worship

Whenever true worship happens, it is because Jesus Christ is in the midst of his people, leading them in their praises and presenting them to the Father as part of his own perfect offering of praise. No matter what form or style our worship may take, no matter what language, instruments, architecture, or art forms we may use—the power of true worship, in all its wonderfully varied manifestations, is *the living Christ in our midst.*

While we sometimes rather glibly speak of worshiping through Christ or praying in the name of Christ, we need to see that it is not just worship or prayer made possible by Christ, but rather it is worship and prayer energized, transported, sanctified, and perfected by Christ as the basis for our acceptance by the Father. This is a much more active understanding of the dynamics of worship and prayer than we often acknowledge. Christ did not just open the way for us to the Father; he doesn't just show us the way to the Father; he *takes us with him* into the Father's presence.

The access of true worship

An obvious (though, in our day, often sadly overlooked) corollary to the truth just above is pointed out by Bob Kauflin:

> No worship leader, pastor, band, or song will ever bring us close to God. . . . Worship itself cannot lead us into God's presence. Only Jesus himself can bring us into God's presence.[18]

Whatever the outward form of our worship may be, there is only *one way* to come to the Father in worship: through Jesus Christ, in the power of the Holy Spirit.

The excellence of true worship

God's accepts and delights in our worship, not because it is so good, so well-rehearsed, so sincere (though all of these things are important), but because our Lord Jesus presents it to the Father in our place and on our behalf—and the Father is *always* pleased with his Son. It is the *Son's* excellence that gains the Father's favor.

---

18. Kauflin, *Worship Matters*, 74.

This is *God's grace for our worship*. He does not intend for us to operate on a performance basis in our worship any more than in our salvation or sanctification. While we should of course offer our best to God in worship (through studying, practicing, and praying), ultimately that is not the ground of our acceptance before him. We cannot impress him with our music! C. S. Lewis warned about our tendency in this regard:

> We must beware of the naive idea that our music can "please" God as it would please a cultivated human hearer. That is like thinking, under the old Law, that He really needed the blood of bulls and goats. . . . For all our offerings, whether of music or martyrdom, are like the intrinsically worthless present of a child, which a father values indeed, but values only for the intention.[19]

God deserves and expects *perfect* worship. He has provided *that* for us in Jesus Christ, as he has in grace provided for our salvation and sanctification also.

> We are accepted by God, not because we have offered worthy worship, but in spite of our unworthiness, because He has provided for us a Worship, a Way, a Sacrifice, a Forerunner in Christ our Leader and Representative. This is the heart of all true Christian worship.[20]

Robert Webber offers us this powerful perspective:

> Who can love God with His heart, mind, and soul?
> Who can achieve perfect union with God?
> Who can worship God with a pure and unstained heart?
> Not me! . . .
> Not you. Not Billy Graham. Not Matt Redman. . . .
> Not anybody I know or you know.
> Only Jesus can. He does for me and for you what neither of us can do for ourselves.
>
> This is the message that is missing in the literature of contemporary [and most other] worship. It is too much about what I ought to do and too little about what God has done for me. God has done for me what I cannot do for myself. He did it in Jesus Christ. Therefore my worship is offered in a broken vessel that is in the process of being healed, but is not yet capable of fullness of joy, endless intense passion, absolute exaltation, and celebration. But

---

19. Lewis, "On Church Music," 98–99).

20. James Torrance, "The Place of Jesus Christ in Worship," in Anderson, *Theological Foundations for Ministry*, 352.

PART 5. JESUS AND OUR WORSHIP

> Jesus, who shares in my humanity yet without sin, is not only my Savior—He is also my complete and eternal worship, doing for me, in my place, what I cannot do.... He is eternally interceding to the Father on our behalf. And for this reason, our worship is always in and through Christ....
>
> Thanks for Jesus Christ, who is my worship. We are free! And in gratitude, we offer our stumbling worship in the name of Jesus with thanksgiving.[21]

ALL OF GRACE

God receives great glory by providing for us what he demands from us. That's grace! The all-sufficiency of Christ envelops, enriches, fulfills, and perfects our worship.

> God does not throw us back upon ourselves to make our response to His Word. But graciously He helps our infirmities by giving us Jesus Christ and the Holy Spirit to make the appropriate response for us and in us.[22]

> I have been crucified with Christ. It is no longer I who live, but Christ who lives in me. And the life I now live in the flesh I live by faith in the Son of God, who loved me and gave himself for me. (Gal 2:20)

SEE ALSO:

Ron Man, *Proclamation and Praise: Hebrews 2:12 and the Christology of Worship*
Reggie Kidd, *With One Voice: Discovering Christ's Song in Our Worship*

[*Worship Notes* 1.6, August 2006]

---

21. Webber, "Contemporary Music-Driven Worship: A Blended Worship Response," in Basden, *Exploring the Worship Spectrum*, 130).

22. Torrance, "The Place of Jesus Christ in Worship," in Anderson, *Theological Foundations for Ministry*, 359.

3

Towards a Christology of Worship

1. The living Christ is present in our midst when we gather for worship.

   "In the midst of the congregation I will sing your praise." (Heb 2:12b)

2. Only in and through Christ can we enter into God's presence in worship.

   There is one Mediator between God and men, the man Christ Jesus. (1 Tim 2:5)

3. Our worship is pleasing and acceptable to God not because of its own excellence, but because of (and only because of) the excellence of his Son. God accepts and delights in our worship, not because of our efforts or our artistry or even our spirituality, but because of the Son's continual offering of worship in our place and on our behalf.

4. The Word of God, by which Christ proclaims his Father's name to his brethren, deserves priority and centrality in our worship.

   "I will tell of your name to my brethren." (Heb 2:12a)

   How are they to believe in him whom they have never heard? . . . Faith comes from hearing, and hearing through the word of Christ. (Rom 10:14, 17)

5. The corporate praise of God's people, led by Christ himself, is an integral and crucial part of the gathering of the church.

PART 5. JESUS AND OUR WORSHIP

> Let the word of Christ dwell in you richly, with all wisdom teaching and admonishing one another with psalms, hymns and spiritual songs; with grace singing to God in your hearts. (Col 3:16)

6. No matter how they may differ in the externals, all true expressions of worship share in common that they are led and mediated by Christ in the power of the Holy Spirit.

   > Through him [Christ] we both have our access in one Spirit to the Father. (Eph 2:18)

   > For we are the true circumcision, who worship in the Spirit of God and glory in Christ Jesus and put no confidence in the flesh. (Phil 3:3)

7. When we preach or lead worship, we do so representing Christ whose ministry it is. He's the preacher; he's the worship leader.

   > "I will tell of your name to my brethren; in the midst of the congregation I will sing your praise." (Heb 2:12)

8. Because Christ leads us in our worship, we can enter boldly and confidently into God's presence.

   > Therefore . . . since we have a great priest over the house of God, let us draw near with a true heart in full assurance of faith." (Heb 10:19, 21–22)

9. By his grace God has provided in Christ the worship he requires of us.

   > "Grant me what You command, and command what You will." (Augustine, *Confessions* X,31).

10. Our singing Savior shows us the appropriateness and necessity of our own songs of praise.

    > "In the midst of the congregation I will sing your praise" (Heb 2:12b).

    > "I will praise you among the Gentiles, and sing to your name" (Rom 15:9).

If Christ our Mediator deems it fitting to sings the Father's praises in the midst of the congregation (Heb 2:12) and among the nations (Rom 15:9), how can we do less?

11. We need to repent of doing worship in our own strength.

> Through, with and in Christ we turn away in penitential self-denial from our own acts of worship and prayer in order to rest in the worship and prayer which our Saviour has already offered and continues to offer to the Father on our behalf.[1]

CONCLUSION

All true worship is in and through and by Jesus Christ. This is a supremely unifying understanding of Christian worship in all times and places and styles and forms.

(adapted from Man, *Proclamation and Praise: Hebrews 2:12 and the Christology of Worship*)

---

1. Thomas Torrance, "Mind of Christ in Worship," 211–12.

4

Worship Leader?
In Search of a Better Title

> Where it appears, the title of "worship leader" should be critiqued, for it suggests a model of worship in which Christ has been displaced from his rightful place. In the Middle Ages it was the priest, now it is the worship leader. Christ's displacement is accentuated by the focus, either implicitly or explicitly, on the leader's personality, charisma and gifts. In this regard, it is noticeable how the leader's casual greeting has replaced the traditional call to worship in many services. It is almost as though the worship leader is the host, welcoming people as he/she would to his/her home.[1]

When I was teaching a conference of young worship leaders in Bangladesh a few years ago, I shared some of the precious truths expounded in the two preceding chapters, then boldly told them *they were not really worship leaders*! Only *Jesus* is; and I told them that our role is more like that of a "worship facilitator."

Imagine my surprise when I saw a banner for that ministry's next worship conference: it was billed as a conference for *worship facilitators*! They had really listened!

To call our role that of worship facilitator is certainly a step in the right direction, and reserves for Jesus the title of Worship Leader, that truly only he can fulfill. But "facilitator" seems a little bland, and doesn't quite capture the richness and privilege of our role.

1. Redding, *Prayer and the Priesthood of Christ*, 298, footnote 30.

However, a friend who is a missionary doing worship ministry in France recently wrote me this:

> I'm doing some practical workshops for a church in northern France this weekend. They call their group of musicians and leaders their *"serviteurs du culte"* (worship servants) which is both original and quite appropriate!

Appropriate indeed! Worship *servants*—what a great way to look at our role. Serving God in worship, and serving his people in worship!

[*Worship Notes* 20.3, March 2025]

PART 6

Shaping Corporate Worship

1

Making Our Worship More Trinitarian

APPRECIATING THE CENTRALITY OF THE TRINITY

The members of the Trinity—Father, Son, and Holy Spirit—are all equally God and equally glorious. Yet, remarkably, the different members of the Trinity voluntarily perform different roles: The Father sends the Son (a major theme in the Gospel of John: 4:34; 5:24, 36–38; 6:29; 7:16; etc.); the Son obeys the Father (John 4:34); and the Spirit glorifies Christ (John 16:14).

It is beautiful that the members of the Trinity are so eternally secure in their relationship with one another that there is never any sense of competition or of one claiming superiority over the other. They willingly perform their different roles in order to fulfill the purposes of their one, unified divine will. So the Father gives his only begotten Son (John 3:16); Jesus is willing to submit to the Father (Luke 22:42) and to become human and to die (Phil 2:6–8); and the Spirit points always to Christ.

The central importance of the doctrine of the Trinity cannot be overemphasized:

> In the doctrine of the Trinity beats the heart of the whole revelation of God for the redemption of humanity. Our God is above us, before us and within us.[1]

---

1. Bavinck, *Reformed Dogmatics: God and Creation*, 2:260)

PART 6. SHAPING CORPORATE WORSHIP

> The Trinity is not one doctrine among others, but gives distinctive shape to Christian faith and practice.... The Father, the Son, and the Spirit stride across the chapters of redemptive history toward the goal whose origin lies in an eternal pact between them. We worship, pray, confess, and sing our lament and praises to the Father, in the Son, by the Spirit.... We are adopted as children, not of a unipersonal God, but of the Father, as coheirs with his Son as Mediator, united to the Son and his ecclesial body by the Spirit.[2]

RECOGNIZING THE IMPORTANCE OF THE TRINITY FOR WORSHIP

Horton then goes further to make this concerning observation:

> One of the reasons that many Christians have found little practical relevance of this doctrine for their lives is that our public worship—and therefore private piety—has become increasingly emptied of Trinitarian references.... To the extent that our experience is not Trinitarian, it is not properly Christian.[3]

We simply cannot assume that the people in our pews have a full and nuanced understanding of the Trinity and the different, though complementary, roles each Person plays. Leslie Newbigin wrote that "the ordinary Christian in the Western world who hears or reads the word 'God' does not immediately and inevitably think of the triune Being—Father, Son, and Spirit—but rather of a supreme monad."[4]

Those of us who plan and lead worship need to make sure both that we have an appreciation for and comprehension of trinitarian truth, and that that truth becomes part of the ethos and language our services.

---

2. Horton, *Pilgrim Theology*, 103.
3. Horton, *Pilgrim Theology*, 103-4.
4. Newbigin, *The Open Secret*, 27.

EMBRACING AND RESTING IN THE TRINITARIAN DYNAMICS OF WORSHIP

The Three Persons Active in Our Worship

As has often been pointed out, the prevailing New Testament pattern of worship is that "we worship the Father through the Son in the power of the Holy Spirit." As John Witvliet has put it:

> The Father receives our worship.
> The Son perfects our worship.
> The Holy Spirit prompts our worship.
>
> Trinitarian worship offered to the Father, through Christ, in the Spirit conceives of God as the One who acts "before" us, "within" us, and "alongside" of us to receive, prompt, and perfect our worship—divine action in continuity with both past and future divine actions. Trinitarian pastoral concern calls for helping worshipers sense the grace, beauty, and majesty of this vision.[5]

The Son's Role in Mediating Our Worship

Jesus Christ is the true Leader of our worship: "I will proclaim your name to my brethren; in the midst of the congregation I will sing your praise" (Hebrews 2:12). No worship leader, pastor, worship set, or song can lead people into God's presence. Only Jesus can!

See part 5, chapter 2 for more on this transformative truth; also the extensive treatment in this author's *Let Us Draw Near: Biblical Foundations of Worship* (pages 308–14) and his earlier *Proclamation and Praise: Hebrews 2:12 and the Christology of Worship.*

This marvelous reality takes a lot of pressure off of worship leader and worshiper alike: we do not come to worship in fear that our offering may not be good enough—when we come through Christ, it's always good enough! Worship is not a *work*—it is our grateful *response* through Christ for all that God has freely given us in the Redeemer.

---

5. Witvliet, "Prism of Glory: Trinitarian Worship and Liturgical Piety," in Spinks, *Place of Christ in Liturgical Prayer*, 298.

PART 6. SHAPING CORPORATE WORSHIP

The Spirit's Role in Motivating and Empowering Our Worship

> For we are the circumcision, who worship by the Spirit of God and glory in Christ Jesus and put no confidence in the flesh. (Phil 3:3)

One way to understand this dynamic is to see the Spirit as the connective tissue between the Revelation and Response poles of the biblical pattern of worship. It is the role of the Holy Spirit to take the revelation of God from our minds into our hearts and to draw forth our response.

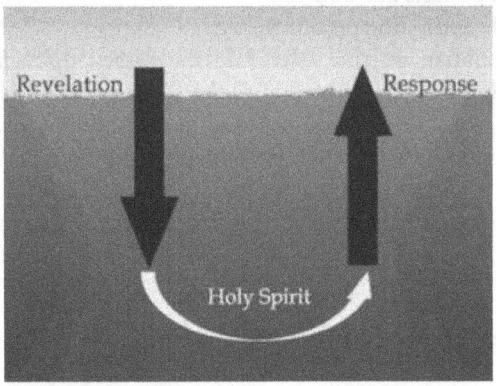

> The "upward" movement of human response in worship . . . is also fundamentally motivated by God. Human response—"the sacrifice of praise and thanksgiving"—arises from the faith that has its source in the indwelling Holy Spirit."[6]

The Spirit takes the *objective* truth about God in Christ and makes it *subjectively* precious to us: objective revelation, subjective response. In this sense, Christ is the *Way* to the Father, but the Holy Spirit is the *Guide*.[7]

Crucially, we can say that we *can* come to the Father because of the ministry of Christ, but we *want* to come to the Father in worship because of the ministry of the Holy Spirit!

---

6. Witvliet, "Prism of Glory: Trinitarian Worship and Liturgical Piety," in Spinks, *Place of Christ in Liturgical Prayer*, 102.

7. "The Holy Spirit subjectively actualizes in us Christ's objective work for us" (Eugenio, *Communion*, 136).

PRACTICING THE TRINITARIAN DYNAMICS OF WORSHIP

> The doctrine of the Trinity is the foundation for several criteria that can be used to evaluate and prescribe liturgical practices in many contexts. These criteria can be phrased as simple questions: Does liturgy speak of God with reference to particular actions in history recorded in Scripture? Does corporate worship in a particular congregation rehearse the whole of the divine economy? Are its liturgical actions carried out as means for a personal relationship and encounter with God? Do these actions acknowledge the example and mediation of Jesus Christ and the inspiration of the Holy Spirit? Does the community itself model the kind of intimate fellowship or koinonia that is central both to divine life and the Christian life? . . . The doctrine of the Trinity . . . is about reconceiving the purpose and meaning of the entire grammar of the liturgical event, reconsidering how we approach God.[8]

Framing the Service from the Outset

It has been recommended that we regularly start our services with some explicit reference to the Trinity whom we have gathered to worship. This may be done in different ways:

1. Making a statement such as "We have gathered here today to worship God, who is Father, Son, and Holy Spirit" or "We have come to worship the Father through the Son in the power of the Holy Spirit" or "We enter the presence of God through our Mediator and High Priest, the Lord Jesus Christ, as the Spirit empowers us."
2. Singing the Doxology
3. Singing a clearly trinitarian hymn, such as "Holy, Holy, Holy" ("God in three Persons, blessed Trinity") or "Come, Thou Almighty King" (one verse for each Person of the Trinity, followed in verse 4 by praises sung "to the great One in Three"); or a contemporary song such as "How Great Is Our God" (Chris Tomlin) ("The Godhead Three in One, Father, Spirit, Son").
4. Reciting the Apostles' Creed or the Nicean Creed

---

8. Witvliet, "Trinitarian DNA of Christian Worship."

Singing the Doctrine

There have been a number of studies bemoaning the relative lack of trinitarian truth in modern-day worship songs. One is Lester Ruth's "How Great Is Our God: The Trinity in Contemporary Christian Worship Music" in the collection *The Message in the Music: Studying Contemporary Praise and Worship*. And Robin Parry, in his excellent book *Worshipping Trinity: Coming Back to the Heart of Worship*, includes a survey which yielded the shocking results that only 1.4% of the songs he analyzed were fully trinitarian, while 51.1% were what he calls "You, Lord" songs, which refer to God generically without any distinguishing of the Persons or roles! Of course, not every song has to include explicit references to the Persons of the Trinity, but the problem has been in the other direction.

These two studies are dated, but still highlight trends which continue in many churches. However, there has been some real improvement in recent years, with some notable trinitarian additions to the contemporary worship repertoire. See "12 Trinitarian Songs Worth Singing" (https://seedbed.com/12-trinitarian-worship-songs-worth-singing/).

CONCLUSION

A full-orbed, robust Christianity delights in the beauty of the trinitarian nature of our faith and our relationship with God. Let us be sure that our congregations are steeped in this truth in their private and public devotion.

SEE ALSO:

Joan Huyser-Honig, "Trinitarian Worship: This Doctrine Makes a Difference in How You Worship" (https://worship.calvin.edu/resources/articles/trinitarian-worship-doctrine-makes-difference-how-you-worship)

Joan Huyser-Honig, "Contemporary Worship Music Matures: Theologically serious song writers are acknowledging Father, Son, and Holy Spirit in contemporary songs that unite head and heart" (https://worship.calvin.edu/resources/articles/contemporary-worship-music-matures)

[*Worship Notes* 19.9, September 2024]

2

Worship and the Word

The Word of God is of supreme importance in the life of the Christian, containing as it does God's revelation of his Person, his will and his ways. The Word needs to be pored over, ingested into one's mind and heart, meditated on, and acted upon. It is a unique and precious repository of spiritual truth and guidance and encouragement. There is no aspect of the life of the church or of the individual believer that should not be tied to a scriptural mooring and infused with biblical substance (2 Tim 3:16–17). The Bible is indeed "a lamp unto my feet, and a light unto my path" (Ps 119:105).

When Christians gather for corporate worship, it is logical that the Word of God should play a central and dominant role. For since worship involves focusing our thoughts and hearts and voices on the praise of God, in response to his self-revelation and his gracious saving initiative, we of course need that view of God which the Word gives us if our worship is to be "in truth" (John 4:23–24). Our worship can only duly honor God if it accurately reflects what he reveals about himself in his Word.

THE WORD NEGLECTED

That said, the astounding observation has been made as to how little use is made of Scripture in the worship services of most evangelical churches. The irony, of course, is that those who claim most strongly to stand on the Bible have so little of it in their worship! While the sermon of course takes a prominent role in our services, even preaching consists mostly of talking *about* the Scriptures (often after reading just a very few verses). It must be said that liturgical groups (whether on the more liberal or the more conservative end of the spectrum theologically) have probably ten times as much actual Scripture in their services (because it is built into their liturgies) as most evangelical free churches!

In too many of our churches the entire first part of the service consists just of music, and no Scripture is read at all. This author has experienced this often, in both traditional and contemporary services (and around the world, for that matter): the problem is pervasive. It would seem crucially important for believers and unbelievers alike to hear at the beginning of a service (and/or see printed in a bulletin or flashed on a screen) verses of Scripture chosen to give a clear signal that: "We have come to worship God. The Word is how we know about God, and therefore it is the foundation for all that we do here and for our understanding of why we have come together." Without such a declaration, worshipers may make the faulty assumption (consciously or unconsciously) that we invite ourselves into God's presence, when in actuality it is only by virtue of his invitation (and his opening the way through the work of Christ) that we may come before him at all.[1]

GIVING THE WORD ITS DUE

As James White puts it, "the first step toward making our worship more biblical is in giving the reading of God's Word a central role in Christian worship on any occasion."[2] We simply cannot overstate the importance of Scripture for our worship. If the God of the universe wants to speak to his gathered people through his Word, we need to listen!

By all means, let us be as creative as possible in building in Scripture (verses on banners or projected onto a screen as people enter, verses on the bulletin cover, readers' theater, children reciting verses, original Scripture songs, etc.). Let us make sure that the primacy of the Word in worship

---

1. "Also interesting to observe is the role of the 'worship team,' usually consisting of a music group, whose task it is to open worship with a 'worship time.' This consists of a bracket of worship choruses, interspersed with the leader's exhortations, humorous asides and extempore prayers. A lot of effort goes into creating the right atmosphere. Music has come to assume a kind of priestly role in much worship, insofar as it is regarded almost as the primary vehicle by which people enter the presence of God" (Redding, *Prayer and the Priesthood of Christ*, 298, footnote 30).

2. White, "Making Our Worship More Biblical," 38.

is obvious throughout the entire service—not just during the sermon. As White adds:

> Scripture is read, not just for a sermon text, but to hear what word God addresses to the gathered congregation. Preaching usually builds on that but Scripture is read for its own sake as God's Word . . . . It needs to be communicated to all that the centrality of Scripture stems from its function as proclamation of God's Word to the gathered people.[3]

The Word and the Prerequisites for Worship

The Word of God helps to bring us to the point where our approach to God in worship is possible: it teaches us that we are dead in our trespasses and sins (Eph 2:1); it reveals that God has provided for redemption, forgiveness, and eternal life through the work of Jesus Christ; and it presents the opportunity to come by faith into a right relationship with the Father. "The washing of water with the Word" (Eph 5:26) provides the spiritual cleanliness which God requires for us to be able to enter confidently into his presence (Ps 15:1–2; Heb 10:19–22; 12:18–24).

The Word as the Inviter to Worship

God has done everything to make our approach in worship possible, and in his Word he extends the invitation (yea, command) to draw near (Heb 10:22). The Old Testament book of worship, the Psalter, is replete with calls to "praise the Lord!" (Hebrew *hallelujah*). As the Danish hymn (text by Thomas Kingo, 1634–1703), puts it:

> We come, invited by your Word,
> To kneel before your altar, Lord.

The Word as the Authority for Worship

The fact of the matter is that every aspect of the service should serve to reflect and honor the Word of God. The sermon (and the preacher) must be subservient to the Word: the Word must guide and control the preacher's

---

3. White, "Making Our Worship More Biblical," 38.

thoughts and words if the sermon is to communicate God's message and not just the ideas of man. But also the music must be subservient to the Word: the texts must reflect and express biblical truth, and the music itself must be a suitable medium to carry the text; the musician(s) must also be subservient to the Word in terms of motivation and execution of the music. In addition, prayers and readings must be consistent with biblical teaching, if not actually taken from Scripture. As John MacArthur has put it, "If we are to worship in truth and the Word of God is truth, we must worship out of our understanding of the Word of God."[4]

The Word as the Material for Worship

Gary Furr and Milburn Price have suggested a number of ways in which the revelation of the Word can be communicated in the service, besides the sermon: Scripture readings of all sorts, music (setting Scripture texts, and also faithfully presenting scriptural truth in paraphrased or freely composed form), symbols (fish, cross, stained glass, etc.), carefully used drama.[5] When Scripture and scriptural truth are pervasive in the service, then the acts of response will properly be understood as response to God's self-revelation through his Word.

The Word as the Regulator of Worship

Worship must be guided and channeled by truth, i.e., be in accordance with what God has revealed about himself and his ways (and, as John 4:25–26 shows, must be through the Son, the Messiah, who is the truth [John 15:6]). As Furr and Price state: "This is the perfect blend: emotion regulated by understanding, enthusiasm directed by the Word of God."[6]

The Word and the Message of Worship

Preaching is part of worship, and leads to worship. Indeed, John Piper calls preaching "expository exultation" and adds: "The all-pervasive, all-important, all-surpassing reality in every text is God. Whether he is commanding

---

4. MacArthur, *The Ultimate Priority*, 122–23.
5. Furr and Price, *The Dialogue of Worship*, 8–14.
6. Furr and Price, *The Dialogue of Worship*, 25.

or warning or promising or teaching he is there. And where he is, he is always supreme. And where he is supreme he will be worshiped."[7]

The Word and the Goal of Worship

The Word should rightly be exalted in our worship (because it is the Word of God), but not as an end in itself. For the ultimate goal of worship (and of the church and of our lives as believers) is to display and proclaim and magnify the glory of God. The glory of God will be well served in our worship as the Word speaks of the wonders of his person and his ways—through reading, preaching, praying, singing, meditating, and practicing ordinances which are infused with and reflective of scriptural truth. The Word will enable us to obey its own command to "praise him according to his excellent greatness" (Ps 150:2).

> You cannot read too much Scripture;
> and what you read you cannot read too carefully,
> and what you read carefully you cannot understand too well,
> and what you understand well you cannot teach too well,
> and what you teach well you cannot live too well.[8]

> Since the Bible is the church's source book of knowledge about its salvation, its guidebook for living, and the promise of its destiny, it must be kept central in the church's worship.[9]

> The Bible is not simply read aloud in order to convey information, to teach doctrine or ethics or whatever, though of course it does that too. It is read aloud as the effective sign that all that we do is done as a response to God's living and active word. . . . The place of Scripture in Christian worship means that both in structure and content God's initiative remains primary and all that we do remains a matter of response.[10]

> Worship without theology is bound to degenerate into idolatry; hence, the essential place of Scripture both in public worship and

---

7. Piper, "Preaching as Worship."
8. Luther, *What Luther Says*, 1110.
9. Segler, *Christian Worship: Its Theology and Practice*, 66.
10. Wright, "Freedom and Framework."

private devotion. It is the word of God that evokes the worship of God.... True knowledge of God will always lead us to worship.[11]

[*Worship Notes* 1.6, June 2006]

---

11. Stott, "Worship."

3

The Call to Worship
Giving God the First Word

Robert Nordling of the Calvin Institute of Christian Worship once told the story of taking his five-year-old son Jackson to a young friend's birthday party. Jackson is all dressed up and brimming with excitement and enthusiasm as he rushes into his friend's house to join in the festivities. However, when his father comes to pick him up after the party, Jackson comes out looking dejected and depressed. His father asks, "Jackson, what's the matter? Didn't you enjoy the party?" Jackson responds with a terse, "No." So his father asks, "But you were looking forward to this party so much! Why didn't you have fun?" And Jackson answers, "I didn't get any presents!!" To which Dad can only reply, "But Jackson, it wasn't *your* party!"

The lesson Nordling draws from this real-life parable is all too apparent and convicting. The worship service is, so to speak, *God's* "party," not ours. And we come primarily not to *receive* (though we certainly do that also), but to *give* to God the presents of our faith, our gratitude, our praises, our confessions, the commitment of our hearts.

God is simultaneously the Inviter, the Host, and the Guest of Honor. Coming to God in worship is God's idea, after all, not ours. In fact, we need to recognize that all of our movement toward God occurs because *God acts first*. God always initiates; we can only respond. (See part 2, chapter 1.)

And our primary response is *worship*. In worship we respond in praise to our God for the glory and greatness that he has revealed to us; we respond in thanksgiving to our God for the saving grace that he has lavished upon us; we respond in wonder and delight to our God for the relationship that he has initiated with us.

It is God who invites us to worship. It is his Word which tells us to "come, let us worship and bow down...." (Ps 95:6). God has revealed himself to us and has established a relationship with us by his power and grace. God delights in that relationship and desires (and deserves) our worship as a means of affirming and strengthening our relationship with him. "Worship the Lord with gladness," says the psalmist, "come before him with joyful songs" (Ps. 100:2). Coming to God is not an option for Christians but rather our obedient response to his gracious invitation.

Many worship services begin with either some innocuous words of greeting by the worship leader—focused on the weather or on the size of the crowd or on the pleasure the leader has in seeing the people gathered. "It is almost as though the worship leader is the host, welcoming people as he/she would to his/her home."[1] Or else the service launches right into songs written about or to God.

But the question is, who deserves the first word in worship? The fact is, we have been invited by God himself into his holy presence. He has taken the initiative for that access to be possible through the work of his Son. God doesn't "show up" at worship, as the popular catchphrase goes. As Steve Fry has put it:

> I'm concerned that some of us have perceived worship as a spiritual talisman we employ to get God to show up, rather than seeing worship as a simple response to His grace.... If we perceive worship as a mechanism that triggers his presence, we'll inadvertently focus on the act of worship itself instead of the One we are worshiping—worshiping worship if you will.[2]

Since God is the Inviter, the Host, and the Guest of Honor, shouldn't we hear first from him? Isn't it entirely appropriate to hear a word of invitation and welcome and testimony from God himself as the one who has made our gathering both possible and meaningful? Let us hear first from God through his Word, and then respond to him with our songs, prayers, and words of praise. Let's honor him and his gracious invitation by letting him have the first word.

[*Worship Notes* 3.3, March 2008]

1. Redding, *Prayer and the Priesthood of Christ*, 298, footnote 30.
2. Fry, "Unity, Worship, and the Presence of God."

4

Thematic Worship
A Rich Feast for the People of God

Too often in our services we jump all over the theological map in our progression of songs—moving quickly from, for instance, the holiness of God to the blood of Christ to the Spirit's leading to the beauty of the Lord to my love for him; and, it should be added, this occurs commonly in churches of both the contemporary and the traditional variety. There is obviously nothing wrong with any of the above themes; but there is a legitimate question whether there is time for the worshipper to adequately grasp and focus on and respond to each new theme (as it passes quickly by) with any degree of depth. It's a little bit like dashing through an art museum and maintaining that we have seen all of the paintings!

If fine paintings are not intended to be glanced at casually, but rather contemplated deliberately and meditatively, how much more so the character of God! If indeed our intent in worship is "the public savoring of the worth of God and the beauty of God and power of God and the wisdom of God,"[1] that savoring will take time and attention.

Thematic worship is one way to give the worshiper the opportunity to savor the wonder of God by allowing for ample time for reflection on and response to a particular aspect of God's Person or ways. We may define thematic worship thus:

---

1. Piper, "Worship God!"

PART 6. SHAPING CORPORATE WORSHIP

Thematic worship is a service where a single aspect of God's nature or work is focused on and celebrated, with the various elements of the service chosen to support and develop that theme.

THE ADVANTAGES OF THEMATIC WORSHIP

Thematic worship allows for a single-minded focus on a singular attribute of God or aspect of his truth, giving opportunity for reflection on and response to that theme. It also brings to bear on the service an organizing principle that is inherently more biblical and lofty than an approach whose unity is merely a stylistic one. And the theme supplies the connective tissue that enables the worship planner to blend together music and other elements of widely varying styles and types, yet with a coherence of subject matter that supersedes any individual style.

The goal in worship is to center our thoughts on God and his truth, and to turn our hearts and voices heavenward in grateful response to the wonders of his being. A proper variety and balance of themes used over time can serve a tremendous catechetical function for the congregation. Through a sustained focus of reflection and response in thematic worship, believers receive into the reservoir of their souls rich deposits of truths that have been savored and personalized and responded to with their whole being.

SELECTING A THEME

Ideally the theme will grow out of the central thrust (or at least some aspect) of the pastor's message; this can bring tremendous unity and impact to the service as a whole. However, when the pastor's preparation timetable does not allow sufficient lead time for the worship planner (as is often the case), the corporate praise portion of the service may develop its own independent theme.

Even if your church does not follow the liturgical year, it can be good to focus on certain key events during the year: Christmas and Easter, of course (every church practices thematic worship on these occasions!), but also such events as the ascension of Christ, Pentecost, Advent, and Reformation Sunday.

And certain great themes bear repeating over and over (at least twice a year), such as the holiness of God, the love of God, etc.; and Communion

Sundays are obvious times to focus on such themes as the cross or the blood of Christ.

THE MATERIALS OF THEMATIC WORSHIP

The unifying principle of the theme allows one to successfully incorporate and blend a rich variety of materials. First and foremost, the Bible should define, focus, develop, and reinforce the theme; a scriptural Call to Worship can introduce the theme explicitly or implicitly.

Different songs and hymns that reinforce the theme should be used, as well as Bible readings (unison or responsive) that develop the theme through the power of corporate reading of the Word of God.

While Scripture should of course be the primary source for readings used in worship, we should not neglect other powerful expressions of biblical truth. The creeds, the *Te Deum*, *Pilgrim's Progress*, the *Heidelberg Catechism*, the Anglican *Book of Common Prayer*, *Valley of Vision* (a wonderful collection of Puritan prayers), and many other sources may be drawn upon to help develop the theme.

Different forms of prayerful response may be appropriately used in the service as well.

And visual and other aids may be used to help in driving home the thematic focus: a banner, artwork, or symbolic object (a shepherd's crook, for instance) may suggest or even make explicit the theme. A title that hints at or names the theme may be put as a heading in the bulletin or on the screen.

WORTH THE EFFORT!

Admittedly, thematic worship takes a significant amount of time and planning. It takes effort to weave together various materials into a smoothly flowing service that develops the theme with appropriate pace and impact. But the potential for genuine worship to God's glory and spiritual fruit in the lives of our people make it worth the effort.

PART 6. SHAPING CORPORATE WORSHIP

EXAMPLES OF POSSIBLE WORSHIP THEMES
AND CORRESPONDING SERVICE TITLES
(used 1990-2000 at First Evangelical Church, Memphis, Tennessee)

SERVICE THEME	SERVICE TITLE(s)
Adoration	Worship and Adore the Lord Our God
Advent	Born to Set Thy People Free
Alleluia	Alleluia! Praise the Lord!
Ascension	Seated at God's Right Hand
Assurance	Blessed Assurance /I Am His. and He Is Mine
Bible	Sweeter Than Honey
Church	Many Members, One Body
Communion	The Body and the Blood
Consecration	I'll Live For Him Who Died For Me
Creation	The Work of Your Fingers/My Father's World
Cross	My Glory All the Cross
Death of Christ	The Blood Applied
Emmanuel	God With Us
Exaltation	Worshipping the Exalted Christ
Faithfulness	Thy Great Faithfulness
Father's Day	Fatherhood: Divine and Human
Glory	To The Praise of His Glory
Grace	Tune My Heart to Sing Thy Grace
Heaven	Join the Everlasting Song/Emmanuel's Land
Heavenly Worship (Rev 4 & 5)	The Praises of Men and Angels
Holiness	Holy Is the Lord!
Holy Spirit	The Comforter Has Come
Jesus	The Praise of Jesus
Jewish	Praising the God of Abraham
Joy	Come With Joyful Singing!
King	King of Kings
Lamb	The Worthy Lamb
Light	The Dawn of Redeeming Grace
Lord	Jesus Is Lord
Love	Amazing Love!
Majesty	The Majesty of His Glory
Mercy	Rest for the Weary
Missions	Striving Together for the Faith of the Gospel
Name of Jesus	No Other Name
Patriotic	Great God of Nations
Power of God	Almighty!
Praise	To God All Praise and Glory!
Prayer	Sweet Hour of Prayer
Presence	Seeking the Face of God
Redeemer	My Great Redeemer's Praise
Reformation	Faith of our Fathers
Resurrection	My Redeemer lives!
Rock	Safe to the Rock
Salvation	Who Shall Ascend?
Sanctity of Life	Precious in His Sight
Savior	Hallelujah! What A Savior!
Second Coming	The King is Coming
Shepherd	The Good Shepherd
Sing	Come before His Presence with Singing
Thanksgiving	Giving Thanks
Thirst	Water for the Soul
Worship	Worthy of Worship

[*Worship Notes* 3.4, April 2008]

5

"In Remembrance of Me"

In obedience to Jesus' command (Luke 22:19),[1] his church has always made the ritual remembrance of his substitutionary sacrifice on the cross a central part of gathered worship. In fact, in most traditions the Lord's Supper was celebrated weekly for the first 1500 years of the church. Some groups continue this practice, though many groups now opt for a monthly observance, while others do it quarterly or even less often. In the absence of specific biblical instruction as to frequency, there is freedom in this respect.

> The Lord's Supper is a powerful showing forth of the life and death, the resurrection and ascension of Christ... The Bible calls us to take and eat and drink as well as to hear.[2]

> We do not come before God in the Eucharist on the ground of what we have done.... We come with nothing in our hands but the bread and wine, to feed upon Christ's Body and Blood and find shelter in His sacrifice and oblation on our behalf.... We do not have to keep looking over our shoulders to see whether our response is good enough. The very fact that in our response we are called to rely entirely upon the steadfast and incorruptible response of Christ made on our behalf frees us from the anxieties

---

1. In fact, Darrell Johnson has pointed out that "eat and drink are the only verbs of worship explicitly commanded by Jesus" (back cover endorsement of Smith, *Holy Meal*).
2. White, "Making Our Worship More Biblical," 40.

begotten of ulterior motivation and evokes genuine freedom and joy in our responding to God.[3]

REMEMBRANCE

An understanding of the biblical nuance of "remembrance" (Greek *anamnesis*) is key to our understanding of the Lord's Supper. James Torrance explains this concept well:

> The word *anamnesis* . . . is of rich liturgical significance in the Bible. It does not mean simply an act of recollection of some remote date of bygone history, as every schoolboy remembers 1066 A.D. Rather it means remembering in such a way that we see our participation in the past event and see our destiny and future as bound up with it. So when Jews remember the passover and the exodus from Egypt, they do not think of it simply as an irretrievable date from over 3000 years ago. Rather they remember it in such a way that they confess "We are the people whom God brought out of the land of Egypt for *we* were Pharaoh's bondmen." "We are the people with whom God made His covenant, saying 'I will be your God and you shall be my people.'"
>
> In cultic remembrance . . . the past is rendered present; there is a re-presentation of the past so that it lives again in the present time. This, for lack of a better word, we may call a presentifying of the past. . . . So at the Last Supper, we do not merely remember the Passion of our Lord as an isolated date from 1900 years ago. Rather we remember it in such a way that we know that we are the people for whom our Saviour died and rose again. We are what we are today by the grace of God because of what God did for us then.[4]

PERSPECTIVES ON THE LORD'S SUPPER

Gordon T. Smith, in an insightful little book entitled *A Holy Meal: The Lord's Supper in the Life of the Church*, unpacks seven perspectives gleaned from the major New Testament passages dealing with the Supper—seven angles from which to observe and understand the practice. Each perspective

---

3. Thomas Torrance, "Word of God and the Response of Man," 158.

4. James Torrance, "The Place of Jesus Christ in Worship," in Anderson, *Theological Foundations for Ministry*, 10, 355–56.

and passage he summarizes with a single key word that is the focus of the passage:

- *Remembrance*: The Lord's Supper as a Memorial (1 Cor 11:24–26)
- *Communion*: The Lord's Supper as Fellowship with Christ and with One Another (1 Cor 10:14–17; 11:27–34)
- *Forgiveness*: The Lord's Supper as a Table of Mercy (Matt 26:26–28)
- *Covenant*: The Lord's Supper as a Renewal of Baptismal Vows (Mark 14:22–25)
- *Nourishment*: The Lord's Supper as Bread from Heaven (John 6:35–58)
- *Anticipation*: The Lord's Supper as a Declaration of Hope (Luke 22:14–27)
- *Eucharist*: The Lord's Supper as a Joyous Thanksgiving Celebration (Acts 2:46–47; also Matt 26:27; Mark 14:23; Luke 22:17, 19; 1 Cor 11:24)[5]

THE SCOPE OF THE LORD'S SUPPER

Time (past-present-future)

At the Table we are reminded of the event of Christ's crucifixion, but in its remembrance we draw comfort from the realization that when Jesus died, he died for each of us—thus bringing the significance of the *past* event into our *present* experience.

There is also a crucial *future* aspect as well. Paul writes: "For as often as you eat this bread and drink the cup, you proclaim the Lord's death until he comes." (1 Cor 11:26) We look ahead to when we will eat, drink, and enjoy table fellowship with our Savior in the kingdom. (Luke 22:16, 18)

> The really distinctive thing about [the Lord's Supper] . . . is its essentially historical and eschatological character. Looking back to an event of the past, it looks forward to the consummation of God's design; and in the present, at each celebration, it finds a creative meeting of the two.[6]
>
> The [ordinances], as Calvin used to say, bear witness to the fact that Christ is in a manner present and yet in a manner absent. But

---

5. Smith, *A Holy Meal*, 35–108.
6. Moule, *Worship in the New Testament*, 19.

when Christ is finally present in the Parousia we shall no longer need [ordinances]—although we shall still worship.[7]

Senses

Of all Christian worship practices, the Lord's Supper is the most multisensory: we hear "the old, old story of Jesus and his love"; we see, touch, smell, and taste the elements.

Emotions

The Lord's Supper is a serious time, but ultimately not a sad one. It is not a funeral service for Jesus! Rather we somberly remember the price paid for our redemption (1 Cor 6:20), yet acknowledge that the work is finished (John 19:30) and that Jesus is our victorious and risen Savior (Rom 1:4), having conquered sin and death (Rom 8:2).

So there is room in the celebration for serious reflection, but also for overwhelming joy and gratitude.

Personal but Corporate

Participating in the Lord's Supper offers the opportunity for *personal* reflection about one's former state and the glorious reality of all that we are and all that we have because we are in Christ by his redeeming work. And it provides the reminder that in Christ all of our sins (including our latest ones!) are forgiven thanks to his shed blood.

Yet at the same time the Lord's Supper is a uniquely *corporate* observance. Many of the activities of worship we can also do when we are alone (Bible study, prayer, even singing); but the Lord's Supper is something we do *together* in the body of Christ.

Churches should consider ways to give attention to this corporate aspect during the celebration of the Lord's Supper: perhaps by singing together as the elements are served; by serving one another the elements; by looking at our neighbor and reminding him or her as we partake that "this is the body/blood of Christ, given for you."

---

7. James Torrance, "The Place of Jesus Christ in Worship," in Anderson, *Theological Foundations for Ministry*, 364.

PART 6. SHAPING CORPORATE WORSHIP

Much more could be said about the wide range of doctrinal understandings and practices of the Lord's Supper among various Christian groups, and there are many books that address these issues. For a balanced overview, please see Chapter 50 in Wayne Grudem's *Systematic Theology*.

[*Worship Notes* 17.3, March 2022; 17.4, April 2022]

PART 7

Church Dynamics

1

The Importance of Worship in the Church

Among undoubtedly others, the following are some of the key purposes of corporate worship:

1. Worship in the church honors the Father.

    This is the ultimate purpose of corporate worship, an end in itself. It serves no higher purpose than this; it is a means to no other end. "Of all the activities in the church, only one is an end in itself: worship."[1]

    God seeks, delights in, and indeed demands our worship. In the corporate gathering we "ascribe to the Lord the glory due his name" (Ps 29:2; 96:8), as we acclaim him as Creator and Ruler, celebrate his supreme worthiness, majesty and attributes, and affirm "there is none like you, and there is no God besides you" (2 Sam 7:22). We exclaim our wonder at his grace and his great plan for the redemption of mankind.

2. Worship in the church celebrates Christ.

    We exalt in the person and work of Christ. We bask in the glory of the gospel, as we tell the "old, old story of Jesus and his love," again and again. And we commemorate his atoning death on the cross, and

---

1. Piper, "Worship Is an End in Itself."

remind ourselves of our part in his redemptive work, as we celebrate the Lord's Supper.

3. Worship in the church facilitates fellowship with Christ and with the Father.

   In corporate worship we draw near to God through, in, and with our Mediator, the Lord Jesus Christ. He grants us access to the Father: and he takes us with him into the Father's presence (Heb 10:19–22) as he actively leads us in our expressions of praise (Heb 2:12).

4. Worship in the church foreshadows the Kingdom.

   Corporate worship reflects the worship of heaven as it looks forward to the time when all creation will continually praise its Maker, when we will "see him as he is" (1 John 3:2), and when we will eat and drink anew with Christ (Luke 22:15–18). The church's worship is a reflection of (and even joining in with) the worship which even now goes on around the throne of God in heaven (Rev 5), and of that ultimate, unending worship in the future.

5. Worship in the church is used by the Holy Spirit.

   In corporate worship the Spirit can act in believers' hearts through the truths proclaimed and sung and prayed, to encourage and engender deeper commitment to and growth in the Lord.

   And unbelievers can also be drawn to the Lord as they watch Christians in worship (1 Cor 14:24–25).

6. Worship in the church gives identity to the church.

   A church is truly and identifiably a church when it is gathered for corporate worship. It is there that we are reminded that we are not *of* the world (John 17:14–16)—we are set apart. And we celebrate our unity in the removal of sociological and ethnic barriers (Gal 3:28).

   And yet we are also reminded that we are still *in* the world (John 17:17–18): we are indeed not in church all the time, but have a necessary missionary aspect to our lives as we go out into the world. A helpful comparison is that of breathing: we breathe in (like the church gathering), and we breathe out (like the church scattering into the world); the process repeats itself over and over and over again. A healthy body must both breath in and out; so too a healthy church body must both gather and scatter.

7. Worship in the church testifies to the world.

    Corporate worship is a *challenge* to a world system that denies the relevance or even the existence of God. We proclaim in our gatherings that this is true reality—the hope of the present and the world's future.

    But corporate worship is not just a challenge to the world, but also an *invitation*: for all are invited to come and taste that the Lord is good, to find redemption and meaning.

8. Worship in the church nurtures the character of the believer.

    We become like that which we worship (Ps 115:8; 135:18). Corporate worship in spirit and truth feeds and nourishes us in the Lord, and fosters our growth in Christlikeness (2 Cor 4:18).

9. Worship in the church builds Christian community.

    We do not gather to each have our own little private worship time with the Lord (there are other places and times for that). But rather together we build ourselves up: as we exercise our gifts for the common good (Eph 4:13–16); as we demonstrate love, kindness, humility, etc., towards one another in the corporate gathering (Col 3:12–15); and as we "let the word of Christ dwell in [us] richly, teaching and admonishing one another in all wisdom, singing psalms and hymns and spiritual songs" (Col 3:16).

    We are also reminded that we are part of universal body of Christ, joining with believers from across the world and across the centuries.

10. Worship in the church reorients believers to their true Center.

    After a week of bombardment by competing worldviews and a panoply of false "worships," corporate worship among God's people reminds us of who, and Whose, we are.

11. Worship in the church prepares hearts for the preaching of the Word.

Of course preaching is part of worship as well (see John Piper, *Expository Exultation*), but it is more of a listening (and responding) activity for the congregation.

As our hearts are filled with wonder from the rehearsal of familiar truths through Scripture readings, songs and prayers, we become more ready to be challenged through the Word preached to ascend to new levels of understanding and commitment.

1.-7. adapted from Jean-Jacques von Allmen, *Worship: Its Theology and Practice.*
8.-9. adapted from Marva Dawn, *Reaching Out without Dumbing Down*, chapters 6 & 7).

[*Worship Notes* 15.1, January 2020]

2

Managing Worship Change

The "worship reformation" of recent years has led many churches to make changes in their worship styles and practices. That is no small matter, and the way is full of potholes and pitfalls. Therefore, how we go about it may be more important (and say more about us) than the results.

GUIDING PRINCIPLES

Here are some suggested principles to help guide the process:

1. The principle of *Scripture*

   The Bible may not give us all the details we need, but it should certainly be our starting point. It gives us the tracks to run on, and we dare not take off "cross-country" into uncharted territory, or we will most certainly end up in a train wreck.

2. The Reformation principle of *semper reformanda* ("always reforming")

   We should always be evaluating our worship practices in light of Scripture. That may or may not lead us to make changes in our practice of worship, but Scripture should always be the final determinant.

   Along those lines, we need also to be reminded that, as R. C. Sproul has put it, the Reformers "were interested, not in innovation, but in renovation. They were reformers, not revolutionaries."[1] What the Reformers had in mind was not novelty, not plowing new ground; rather they stressed the need for continual mid-course corrections to bring our practice back more clearly in line with Scripture.

Let us indeed apply all the creative forces at our disposal to make our worship more interesting, exciting, inspiring—but in a way which is profoundly true to Scripture.

3. The principle of *purposeful change*

It is so important not to undertake change simply for change's sake. That is not a worthy goal. Any change in our worship must be motivated by a sincere desire to enhance the worship of Almighty God. As Gordon Borror and Ron Allen said in their ahead-of-its-time book *Worship: Rediscovering the Missing Jewel* (1982), we must be a people "more committed to God than to change."[2]

This is where the leadership of the church has a great responsibility to lead in a godly way. Bryan Chapell has stressed that a church's leaders must be "sitting together and saying: 'This is the community that God has called us to minister to. How can we best work here for the glory of God and the good of His people?'"[3]

4. The principle of *unity*

In our age of rampant individualism and a pervasive "what's in it for me?" mentality, there must be a deep commitment, on the part of the leadership and the congregation, to avoid pursuing a course of worship change which alienates or disenfranchises one segment of the people in the process. The point is not for one group to "win" and get what it wants; the point is for God to get what he wants. And he wants every believer to love self-sacrificially and to sublimate one's own desires for the good of the whole. How we need that kind of Christlikeness to pervade our modern-day worship debates! It's an issue of maturity, of a godly perspective which chooses "deference over preference."[4]

---

1. Sproul, *Grace Unknown*, 28.
2. Borror and Allen, *Worship*, 189.
3. Chapell, *Christ-Centered Worship*, 132.
4. A favorite saying of the late Chip Stam.

Worship in a congregation racked with disunity is hardly pleasing to God—in fact, it is hard to see how it can be worship at all (see Matt 5:23–24).

5. The principle of *instruction*

   Once the leadership has determined a course for the church to take (after much listening to the people), they should deliberately, thoughtfully, and comprehensively explain the purpose behind the change(s), being especially careful to show its biblical moorings. The people must be told the *why*, not just the *what* of the anticipated change. (This assumes, of course, the kind of purposeful change described in #3 above.)

6. The principle of *incrementalism*

   Nothing has been historically more messy than an over-enthusiastic new pastor deciding to make radical changes in a church's worship overnight; that consistently ends in disaster for the church. A proper concern for the unity of the body will recognize the wisdom of "making haste slowly." Gradual change gives the people time to make adjustments to new practices; going slowly honors the overriding goals of true worship and unity.

7. The principle of *prevailing prayer*

   We cannot possibly know all the issues or foresee all the dangers in pursuing worship change. And so we need to beg God for his wisdom and guidance (Rom 8:26–27; Jas 1:5).

CONCLUSION

The great Reformer John Calvin himself saw the need both for purposeful change in worship, and for great care in pursuing it:

> [The Master] did not will in outward discipline and ceremonies to prescribe in detail what we ought to do (because he foresaw that this depended on the state of the times, and he did not deem one form suitable for all ages) . . . Because he has taught nothing specifically, and because these things are not necessary to salvation, and for the upbuilding of the church ought to be variously

accommodated to the customs of each nation and age, it will be fitting (as the advantage of the church will require) to change and abrogate traditional practices and to establish new ones. Indeed, I admit that we ought not to charge into innovation rashly, suddenly, for insufficient cause. But love will best judge what may hurt or edify; and if we let love be our guide, all will be safe.[5]

Wise advice, indeed!

[*Worship Notes* 17.1, January 2022]

---

5. Calvin, *Institutes*, IV, 10, 30.

3

The Pastor and Worship

THE PASTOR'S VITAL ROLE IN THE WORSHIP LIFE OF THE CONGREGATION

Worship is central to the identity and the life of the body of Christ, including of course corporate worship, as Eduard Schweizer affirms: "Public worship is clearly and openly the place in the congregation's life at which it manifests itself as the Body of Christ."[1] Similarly, William Willimon states: "[Corporate] worship is the center of the Christian community's upbuilding. . . . In worship, all the community's concerns meet and coalesce."[2]

As a result, every pastor should see corporate worship life as an important part of his spiritual oversight of the flock. The pastor has the responsibility of publicly cherishing the glory of God and expounding it and inviting others to share in the wonder of wholehearted, and wholelife, worship. Every pastor should have this ultimate vertical purpose to his ministry: a purpose of seeking to see the glory of God reflected in the lives of his people; a praying and striving towards a preoccupation with God; a loving of him with all the soul, heart, mind, and strength, on his own part as well as that of the congregation; a private and public cherishing of him in

---

1. Schweizer, "Worship in the New Testament," 205.
2. Willimon, *Worship as Pastoral Care*, 20.

lives of worship. *Ultimately, ministry is the work of seeking, in the power of the Holy Spirit, to build more and better worshipers of God.*

Alas, these goals too often seem elusive in light of what has often been termed the "worship wars" endemic in so many of our churches. As John Witvliet diagnoses: "The Christian church is deeply divided into communities that rehearse different histories and embody divergent aesthetic preferences."[3] And indeed, "a church at war with itself, or divided into neat cells of parties agreeing to disagree, can't do its work very well."[4] The continuing disunity in many evangelical churches over issues of worship highlights the need for pastors to give strong, informed leadership to their congregations in this area, in order to preserve the unity and witness of the body.

A pastor will need to bring a solid biblical and theological understanding to bear on worship discussions in the church, if those discussions are not to degrade into mere wranglings over personal opinions, style preferences, and generational proclivities (as, sadly, they so often do). The pastor will also need a firm grasp of historical and contemporary issues in the ongoing worship debates, and a considerable measure of pastoral and practical wisdom in order to navigate the treacherous waters where so many churches have foundered, to the dishonoring of Christ and his church.[5]

POINTS OF ENGAGEMENT FOR THE PASTOR

1. *Be a private worshiper.* This goes without saying. You cannot lead someone where you have not been yourself. Personal spiritual discipline and nurture is foundational to any ministry in the body of Christ, and certainly for the pastor.

2. *Sing, pray and preach out of a walk of worship.* That is, a life of private worship will, and should, show when one is leading the flock in worship. The pastor's personal and private enrichment cannot help but overflow in a deeper, more relevant, and more engaging manner in leading the service.

---

3. Witvliet, "Trinitarian DNA of Christian Worship: Perennial Themes in Recent Theological Literature."

4. Plantinga and Rozeboom, *Discerning the Spirits*, 118.

5. The above section was excerpted from Man, *Dallas Seminary Worship Preparation for Future Pastors* (DMin dissertation).

3. *Study worship.* As stated above, the pastor should be a student of worship, in order to be able to give solid biblical guidance to the church in its discussions about and practices of worship.

4. *Preach on worship.* The fruits of the pastor's study on worship should be shared with the congregation, so that they too can achieve a more balanced understanding of what God says about worship and wants from our worship.

5. *Model worship publicly.* The best example of this I ever saw was when I once attended a service in Fullerton, California, when Chuck Swindoll was the pastor there. It was striking just how personally engaged he was during the entirety of the service (not just the preaching part). Congregants will know what pastors value in the service by watching their level of involvement.

6. *Lead worship.* The pastor should not abdicate all worship leadership to the worship pastor or worship leader. The entire service is to be a ministry of the Word (Col 3:16), and the pastor can help to shape and guide it by being involved both in its preparation and its implementation.

7. *Handle the text reverently and responsively in sermon preparation.* Sermon preparation is an act of worship! Pastors should ask themselves: "What is God showing me about himself in this text? How should I love and praise him more as a result?"

8. *Preach as an act of worship.* Handling God's Word is a serious responsibility, and presenting it to others a holy privilege; when pastors do so they are actively representing Christ, whose ministry it is to "proclaim [the Father's] name to my brethren" (Heb 2:12). (See part 5, chapter 2.)

9. *Preach as an invitation to worship.* As God's spokesman on behalf of his inscripturated Word, pastors open the text to their people so that they can see him, wonder at his excellencies, and humbly bow before his majesty and grace.

[*Worship Notes* 3.10, October 2008]

PART 8

Worship and Culture

1

A Letter from Tapescrew
(with apologies to C. S. Lewis)

My dear Woodworm,

On earth, people are presently in what I like to call the "Do It Yourself" age. Everywhere you look, men and women are in relentless pursuit of independence: financial independence, political independence, independence from responsibility, independence from objective standards of behavior, independence from marriage vows, independence from unwanted pregnancies, independence from all restraints and limitations to their so-called "self-fulfillment" and "self-expression."

Their singers sing, "I did it my way"; their poets proclaim, "I am the master of my fate, I am the captain of my soul"; their business tycoons boast of being "self-made men"; their authors write "self-help" books by the truckload; their commercials insist, "Have it your way . . . you're worth it."

Of course, "DIY" is the foundation of religion, and as such it has been an effective tool for blinding earthly creatures to the Enemy's efforts to buy their release. The root of all sin is independence—independence from the Enemy's claim to one's sole allegiance—and this is, of course, the way our Father in Hell charted for us so long ago.

Naturally we cringe and grieve when any of the miserable creatures actually takes the step of acknowledging ultimate dependence on the Enemy and becomes a Christian. But even then, all is not lost. We can still wreak such havoc as to make them largely ineffective. The spirit of the age, which

PART 8. WORSHIP AND CULTURE

we have so skillfully woven through the very fabric of their society, can infect them and derail them from being constructive agents for the Enemy.

You see, no sooner do these creatures cast their loyalty upon him than we are right back on the job, clogging their minds with the nagging question, "What should I do?" In their compulsion to "get busy for God," they forget (or rather, we drown out) their just-learned dependence on the Enemy and assume that they need to take it from there. And so they do their best to live what they call "the Christian life" in their own strength. It's rather fun to watch them scurry about like ants at a picnic. We are delighted to let them make this futile attempt at self-determination, because they run out of steam pretty quickly. Then they wonder why they sense no victory, why it seems so hard, why they can't get it together. And we gloat, knowing that we have fogged their minds and avoided that dependence on the Enemy's power which is our only true fear.

In a subtle way their worship is similarly infected by the "DIY" mentality. When worship is merely an exercise of self-effort it is, of course, doomed to failure. As long as we keep them trying to impress each other or the Enemy himself with the size, quality, or enthusiasm of their worship activities, there's no real danger of anything profound or eternally significant happening.

It's amusing to sit back and watch the little vermin struggling to "make worship happen," trying to force their way into the Enemy's presence, as though he had to be cajoled into giving them an audience! If they only knew the truth about the power of true worship, we'd be running for cover! But as long as we can keep their focus on what *they do*, rather than on what the Enemy *has done*, they'll be left in a constant state of wondering whether their efforts are good enough.

Having been "saved by grace" as they call it (and how we shudder at those words!), they revert to religion and try to reach the Enemy without ever being quite certain that they will "make the cut." "DIY" worship keeps them guessing, which is the surest way to keep them off-balance—which is, of course, right where we want them! As long as they resist full dependence on God in their worship, and in their walk, they will spin their wheels without making much progress. Exactly what our Father in Hell has in mind.

Affectionately yours,
Uncle Tapescrew

[*Worship Notes* 15.5, May 2020]

2

Another Letter from Tapescrew

My dear Woodworm,

When human creatures first come into the world, they are notorious for their single-minded focus on their basic needs, and their effectiveness in making those needs known. They make it *very* clear to everyone around them that they want what they want, and they want it *now*, and they won't rest until they get it. Delightfully, many of them never seem to advance beyond this stage!

I tell you, we have certainly put that tendency to good use when it comes to their worship services. The "tyranny of taste," I like to call it, or the "power of preference." You see, when they first show up for worship, they may enjoy well enough mingling with others, usually chatting idly and mindlessly about things like the weather or last night's sports scores. But the moment the service starts, "it's every man for himself," as they say. Any thought of community is quickly extinguished as each one prefers instead to see it as an opportunity for some "one-on-one" time with the Enemy.

This perspective causes them to evaluate everything which goes on in the service through their own individual grid. Each one comes with a whole set of personal standards, expectations, hopes, needs, and desires—and they each see worship as a failure if their own agenda is not accomplished. And so we get a delightful cycle of frustration and disappointment and disillusionment which only serves to turn them even more in on themselves.

And of course, when everyone comes to the service with his or her own agenda, they are on a collision course with each other. What one likes, the other despises, and vice versa. It's just marvelous to see that kind of dynamic! Rarely is any pleasure taken in one another's spiritual journey— and we're often able to encourage rather a sort of competitive spirit which guarantees a total lack of community.

This whole area of worship has certainly been worth all of the attention and effort we have given it over the past several years. How like our Father in Hell to so skillfully corrupt something so central as worship in the hearts and minds of the Enemy's people! Would you believe it, we can so fill their minds with disapproving thoughts about the songs or the musicians or the decorations or the lighting, that sometimes they can go through an entire service with hardly a thought about the Enemy himself! And even if they leave with a positive feeling, it's often because of a satisfying personal experience which has stroked their ego but still largely left God out of the picture. How delicious it is that in all our work of seeking to distract them from a heavenly focus, one of our most effective tools should be the worship service itself!!

And so, my dear Woodworm, don't fret yourself about all this attention being given to worship these days: the programs in their churches, the books, the seminars and conferences, the recordings and concerts, the sermon series— this new fad just adds to their busy striving, and leaves them wonderfully ignorant that the worship they're working so hard at is to be found simply through a restful preoccupation with the Enemy himself. As long as we keep them from learning that, we'll be OK.

Stay the course, my dear nephew.

Affectionately yours,
Uncle Tapescrew

[*Worship Notes 7*, July 2020]

[two more Tapescrew Letters, "More from Tapescrew" and "Tapescrew Letter 4," can be found at worship-resources.org/articles-by-rm/]

3

The Bridge
Worship and Culture

Just what is it in the Bible that is supposed to govern and determine our worship? It is a reasonable assumption that the virtual silence of the New Testament writers on the matters of form and style for worship means that the Lord intends for us to have considerable latitude and flexibility in these areas. Yet our worship services still need to look like something—so how are we to make choices? Is it just a case of "anything goes"?

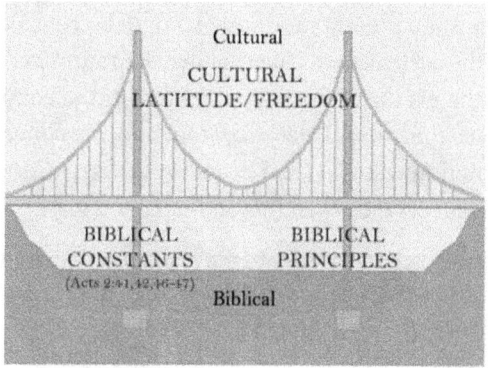

Here is one model which at the same time reflects biblical norms yet allows for biblical freedom. It is based on certain characteristics of a suspension bridge (familiar examples of suspension bridges are the Brooklyn Bridge in New York City and the Golden Gate Bridge in San Francisco).

PART 8. WORSHIP AND CULTURE

In a suspension bridge, the weight is supported by both the towers and the suspension cable. The towers are sunk deep in the earth and are meant to be as stable and immovable as possible. The suspension cable or span, on the other hand, while sharing a significant portion of the load-bearing, nevertheless has by design a great deal of flexibility to expand and contract, thus allowing the bridge to withstand variances in temperature, wind, weight load, etc. It should also be pointed out that, while both the stationary columns and the flexible span are both important parts of the bridge's construction, yet ultimately the cable transfers much of the weight of the road bed and its traffic to the towers, so that the towers are crucial to the bridge's integrity and durability.

What can we then learn about our worship from this illustration? Our worship needs to be supported by firmly rooted biblical foundations, which are illustrated by the two towers. The flexible cable span suggests the liberty that the New Testament seems to allow for individual congregations to constitute their corporate worship. Like any art form, Christian worship allows for much creative expression, but within defined parameters. The Bible gives those parameters as well as that freedom.

THE FIRST TOWER: BIBLICAL CONSTANTS

The first tower suggests an immovable aspect of Christian worship that we could term "Biblical Constants." These are non-negotiables, elements which simply must be present for our worship to be considered Christian.

What are these elements? One clue may be found in Acts 2. Luke has just recounted the events of the day of Pentecost: the coming of the Holy Spirit upon Jesus' followers, Peter's sermon, and the conversion and baptism of "three thousand souls" (2:41). And *in the very next verse*, Luke tells us what these believers did when they gathered together:

> And they devoted themselves to the *apostles' teaching* and *fellowship*, to the *breaking of bread* and the *prayers*. . . . *praising God* and having favor with all the people. (2:42, 47)

The words in italics suggest a list of *normative* activities for the people of God when they congregate together:

1. the Word of God
2. fellowship

3. the Lord's Supper
4. prayer
5. praise

Other necessary elements for worship would be of course a focus on the gospel and on Christ and his work.

THE SPAN: FLEXIBILITY AND FREEDOM

The cable span, with its built-in elasticity and flexibility, represents the freedom that the New Testament seems to allow for wise and prudent application of culturally meaningful expressions (always within the biblical restraints, of course). The "heart language of the people" is be considered when making decisions about forms, styles, music, and other artistic expressions of faith.

We certainly can see the application of this principle (consciously or not) in the vast array of worship expressions seen down through the history of the Christian church, and in churches around the world today. There has been, and is, an enormous variety in terms of architecture, atmosphere, form, structure, style, dress, music, liturgy, etc.

The virtual silence of the New Testament as to the specifics of congregational worship practice seems to allow for a local church, as the fundamental unit of the body of Christ on earth, to have considerable autonomy and freedom in working out the issues involving the balance of biblical constants and cultural flexibility in the worship of that church. That does not mean that it is an easy task, however—as recent history has amply demonstrated. The so-called "worship wars" are symptomatic of the kind of danger into which freedom of this sort can cast us; and we might indeed be left wishing that Paul had just prescribed a set liturgy for all time and left it at that! God obviously wants his people to apply biblical wisdom and discernment in this area, as well as in many other areas where he has chosen not to spell everything out for us.

THE SECOND TOWER: BIBLICAL PRINCIPLES

The New Testament does not give us a lot of specifics about how to do worship in the local congregation; but this most certainly does not mean that we have no biblical guidance concerning worship. It is not "anything goes"! As with so many areas in our lives not specifically addressed by the Scriptures (be it movies, smoking, etc.), there most certainly *are* biblical truths which are applicable and which we must with wisdom and honesty apply to our situation.

There are a host of principles that can be drawn from the pages of Scripture to guide the leadership of local churches in fashioning biblically appropriate yet culturally meaningful expressions of worship. These principles serve as the second tower in our illustration, giving further stability and strength to the worship structure as a whole.

Biblical principles are different than biblical constants because principles must be applied; and they may be applied differently in different situations.

Twelve of these principles are unpacked in part 1 of this book.

CONCLUSION

In today's raging worship debates we desperately need to see that there are biblical constants and principles on which we really can agree. And then we need to have the grace and maturity to allow for the differences in approach that God himself seems to allow for. There is far more that binds us as worshipers than divides us—there is "one body and one Spirit—just as you were called to the one hope that belongs to your call—one Lord, one faith, one baptism, one God and Father of all, who is over all and through all and in all" (Eph 4:4–6).

[*Worship Notes* 2.8, August 2007]

PART 9

The Church Year

Note: Regardless of whether a church follows the entire traditional system of the church year, there are of course key events which can be profitably commemorated and celebrated in our worship services. This part offers studies on some of these important occasions.

GOOD FRIDAY

1

The Power of the Cross
Testimonies from Church History

> But far be it from me to boast except in the cross of our Lord Jesus Christ, by which the world has been crucified to me, and I to the world. (Gal 6:14)

> I am not ashamed of the gospel, for it is the power of God for salvation to everyone who believes, to the Jew first and also to the Greek. (Rom 1:16)

THE POWER OF THE CROSS TO OPEN PARADISE

The thief on the cross (born: ? ✢ born again: 32 A.D.)

CRIMINAL TO CHILD OF GOD

One of the criminals who were hanged railed at Jesus, saying, "Are you not the Christ? Save yourself and us!" But the other rebuked him, saying, "Do you not fear God, since you are under the same sentence of condemnation? And we indeed justly, for we are receiving the due reward of our deeds; but this man has done nothing wrong." And he said, "Jesus, remember me when you come into your kingdom." And he said to him, "Truly, I say to you, today you will be with me in Paradise." (Luke 23:39–43)

THE POWER OF THE CROSS TO CONVERT THE SOUL

Saul/Paul (born c. A.D. 5 ✣ born again: c. A.D. 34)

PERSECUTOR TO EVANGELIST

If anyone else thinks he has reason for confidence in the flesh, I have more: circumcised on the eighth day, of the people of Israel, of the tribe of Benjamin, a Hebrew of Hebrews; as to the law, a Pharisee; as to zeal, a persecutor of the church; as to righteousness under the law, blameless. But whatever gain I had, I counted as loss for the sake of Christ. Indeed, I count everything as loss because of the surpassing worth of knowing Christ Jesus my Lord. For his sake I have suffered the loss of all things and count them as rubbish, in order that I may gain Christ and be found in him, not having a righteousness of my own that comes from the law, but that which comes through faith in Christ. (Phil 3:4b–9a; see also 1 Tim 1:14–15; Acts 9)

THE POWER OF THE CROSS TO GIVE NEW LIFE

Augustine (born: A.D. 354 ✣ born again: A.D. 386)

LIBERTINE TO THEOLOGIAN

I quickly returned to the bench where . . . I had put down the apostle's book [Paul's Epistle to the Romans] when I had left there. I snatched it up, opened it, and in silence read the paragraph on which my eyes first fell: "Not in rioting and drunkenness, not in chambering and wantonness, not in strife and envying, but put on the Lord Jesus Christ, and make no provision for the flesh to fulfill the lusts thereof" [Rom 13:13–14]. I wanted to read no further, nor did I need to. For instantly, as the sentence ended, there was infused in my heart something like the light of full certainty and all the gloom of doubt vanished away." (*Confessions* 8.12)

We glimpse our goal across the sea of the present age.... But to enable us to go there, the One who is our goal came to us.... No one may cross the sea of his age, unless he be carried by the Cross of Christ.... So do not forsake the Cross, and the Cross will carry you. (*Tractates on the Gospel of John*, 2.2)

THE POWER OF THE CROSS TO FREE FROM GUILT

Martin Luther (born: 1483 ✢ born again: 1516)

FEARER TO REFORMER

Though I lived as a monk without reproach, I felt that I was a sinner before God with an extremely disturbed conscience.... I did not love, yes, I hated the righteous God who punishes sinners. Thus I raged with a fierce and troubled conscience.... At last, by the mercy of God, meditating day and night, I gave heed to the context of the words, namely, "In it [the gospel] the righteousness of God is revealed, as it is written, 'He who through faith is righteous shall live'" [Rom 1:17]. There I began to understand that the righteousness of God is that by which the righteous lives by a gift of God, namely by faith.... Here I felt that I was altogether born again and had entered paradise itself through open gates." (*Works*, vol. 34, 336–37)

THE POWER OF THE CROSS TO AMAZE WITH GRACE

John Newton (born: 1725 ✢ born again: 1747)

SLAVE TRADER TO PREACHER

I hope it will always be a subject of humiliating reflection to me that I was once an active instrument in a business at which my heart now shudders. "O to grace how great a debtor . . ." [from "Come Thou Fount of Every Blessing" by Robert Robinson, 1758] ("Thoughts upon the African Slave Trade," 1788)

To be inscribed upon my death: "John Newton, Clerk, once an infidel and libertine, a servant of slaves in Africa, was, by the rich mercy of our Lord and Saviour Jesus Christ, preserved, restored, pardoned, and appointed to preach the faith he had long labored to destroy. (Self-epitaph, on his gravestone in Olney, England)

THE POWER OF THE CROSS TO CONVERT THE MIND

C.S. Lewis (born: 1898 ✤ born again: 1929)

ATHEIST TO APOLOGIST

Really, a young Atheist cannot guard his faith too carefully. Dangers lie in wait for him on every side.... You must picture me alone in that room at Magdalen [College, Oxford University], night after night, feeling, whenever my mind lifted even for a second from my work, the steady, unrelenting approach of Him whom I so earnestly desired not to meet. That which I greatly feared had at last come upon me. In the Trinity Term of 1929 I gave in, and admitted that God was God, and knelt and prayed: perhaps, that night, the most dejected and reluctant convert in all England.... I did not then see what is now the most shining and obvious thing: the Divine humility which will accept a convert even on such terms. The Prodigal Son at least walked home on his own feet. But who can duly adore that Love which will open the high gates to a prodigal who is brought in kicking, struggling, resentful, and darting his eyes in every direction for a chance of escape?... The hardness of God is kinder than the softness of men, and His compulsion is our liberation. (*Surprised by Joy*, chap. 14)

It costs God nothing, so far as we know, to create nice things: but to convert rebellious wills cost him crucifixion. (*Mere Christianity*, chap. 32)

THE POWER OF THE CROSS TO LEAD US HOME

Elderly woman (born: 1923 ✤ born again: c. 1929)

CHILD TO CHILD OF GOD

I was a fortunate little girl. I had a mother and daddy that loved the Lord Jesus, and wonderful Sunday School teachers. And they would keep telling me about God, who made this whole world, became a person to take my place on the cross; and would talk to me about the Lord Jesus, and how he shed his precious blood that cleanses me from all of my sin. And because of this, when I asked Jesus to be my Savior, God forgave me my sin, he made me his child, he brought me into his family, covered me with his righteousness, and gave me his precious Holy Spirit. And all these years the joy of my life has been experiencing the Lord Jesus with me every day. One of my wonderful Sunday School teachers, Mrs. Fanny King, loved the Lord. (You'll meet her when you go to heaven.) She would talk to us about heaven every Sunday and teach us how the Lord Jesus was preparing a place in his glorious home in heaven for all who loved him. And I've been looking forward to going and being with him ever since. In fact, I can hardly wait!

THE POWER OF THE CROSS TO GIVE A NEW BEGINNING

Young man (born: 1989 ✥ born again: 2011)

Darkness to Disciple

I wore rage like a blanket, like a suit of armor that could be put on at any point to deflect relationships and to keep from people getting too close to me. I shunned relationships and I pushed others away, not knowing how it affected them, and definitely not knowing how it affected me. Luckily, I had a group of friends that persevered with me and continually pushed, in a good way, the word of Christ into my life; continually asking me to come to a youth group and to experience something else. Eventually, I felt comfortable enough with them and the people around me to share my story and the fact that I had such rage and such contempt and such anger. And one night I felt it being lifted off of me. I felt it was okay to take down this suit of armor. I felt Christ take it off. With this new beginning, I am able to grow. I am able to foster relationships and love those that had been loving me all along. I am able to persevere through hardship with him at my side; and with those people around me in Christ, I feel like I have become what God wants me to be or continually to grow as God wants me to.

✥

> For the word of the cross is folly to those who are perishing,
> but to us who are being saved it is the power of God. (1 Cor 1:18)

The last two people quoted were members of First Evangelical Church in Memphis, Tennessee. A worship service featuring all of the above testimonies, with musical commentary by the First Evan Worship Choir with orchestra, may be viewed on YouTube by searching "FEC Palm Sunday 2014"; and the program can be found at worship-resources.org/Palm-Sunday.

[*Worship Notes* 10.3, March 2015]

EASTER

2

Easter Sunday and Every Sunday

The resurrection of Jesus Christ is the pivotal point in human history and the focal point of the Church's corporate celebrations. As Laurence Stookey points out in his excellent book *Calendar: Christ's Time for the Church*:

> Christians saw in the resurrection profound evidence of the renewal of the first creation, which had become ruined by human rebellion and thus was alienated from the Creator. Easter was the inauguration of a new era.[1]

The resurrection of Christ was the key affirmation of Christ's finished work and God's acceptance of it for the redemption of humanity (Rom 1:1–4). It was also therefore central to the apostolic proclamation of the gospel; there are 22 references to the resurrection in the book of Acts alone (see the "Resurrection Concordance" in the next chapter).

THE WEEKLY FEAST

However, Stookey urges us not to see Easter (much less Christmas) as the primary celebration of the church. Rather he makes a compelling case that

---

1. Stookey, *Calendar*, 40.

it is *every Sunday* that is the focus of the Christian calendar, as a weekly commemoration of the day of resurrection. Stookey writes:

> It is usually taken for granted that because of the appeal of their liturgical celebrations and due to the general popularity of customs surrounding their observance, Christmas and Easter are the primary feasts of the church. But, in fact, the primary Christian feast must occur weekly, not annually, in order to testify to the way in which the humiliation-exaltation of God in Christ has transformed the totality of human life.[2]

Christ of course rose on a Sunday, and appeared on that day to the women at the tomb (Matt 28:1; Mark 16:2; Luke 24:1; John 20:1), to the two disciples on the road to Emmaus (Luke 24:13), and to the larger group of disciples in the upper room (Luke 24:36); as well as to the disciples again (this time including Thomas) "eight days later" (another Sunday in Jewish reckoning; John 20:26). And Acts 20:7 shows believers gathered together on the first day of the week. Stookey comments:

> In addition to going to the synagogue on the seventh day, the early Christians assembled to rejoice in the resurrection on the first day of the week.[3]

So in emphasizing weekly Sunday worship as the foundational celebration of the church and the church year, Stookey advocates a realignment of the way we look at Easter:

> It has become a maxim of late that "every Sunday is a little Easter." But it would be more accurate to say that . . . "every Easter is a great Sunday," a time, in effect, to reflect more deeply and with a greater degree of sustained concentration upon what the church affirms weekly about the work of God in our midst.[4]

For, as he points out, the Church's central affirmation has always been that "the Lord is risen and at work among us."[5]

---

2. Stookey, *Calendar*, 49.
3. Stookey, *Calendar*, 40.
4. Stookey, *Calendar*, 54–55.
5. Stookey, *Calendar*, 28.

FIRST DAY AND EIGHTH DAY

As the pivotal event in history, and therefore in our annual and weekly observances as Christ's church, the resurrection is a reference point for looking back and looking forward, for remembrance and anticipation:

> On any given Lord's Day, the worshiping church in the present fleeting moment grasps both the past (by commemorating . . . the Lord's resurrection and all that served to prepare for it) and the future (by affirming . . . the fulfilled reign of God, the Day of the Lord). Both of these are present to us as we experience the transforming power of the resurrection in our lives and thereby begin to live even now in the ways of the future. All of time is thus bound together in the day of worship itself.[6]

This understanding is confirmed by the way the early church took the Jewish apocalyptic usage of the term "eighth day," denoting the future age, and applied the concept to Sunday worship. As both the "first day" of the week *and* the "eighth day," Sunday looks back to the fulfillment of God's redemptive promises to a fallen world, and looks ahead to the kingdom, when all will be made new, and to the final summing up of all things in Christ (Eph 1:10). It shows the continuity and the progression in Christ between the first creation and the new creation. As the first of the regular days of the week, Sunday reminds us that we are indeed "in the world"; yet, as the eighth day, it looks to the future and also reminds us that we are not "of the world":

> In the cosmic newness revealed in the resurrection of Jesus Christ we find the promise and foretaste of our own transformation. We are privileged to be participants of the divine nature. Therefore the church celebrates the resurrection of Christ and of the whole creation as the center of a weekly cycle, every Lord's day, and as the center of an annual cycle, every Easter.[7]

Alexander Schmemann helpfully points out that to see Sunday primarily as a day or rest or a "Christian sabbath" is itself a suspect reinterpretation of Old Testament Sabbath law; he points out that for the first three centuries of the church, Sunday was a regular work day, and Christians would have had to gather either early in the morning or late in the evening for worship. (And besides, the Romans did not even follow a seven-day

---

6. Stookey, *Calendar*, 40.
7. Stookey, *Calendar*, 38.

week, that being a Jewish convention.) The focus of Sunday was not on the cessation of activities, but rather a concerted labor of celebration and worship in commemoration of the Lord's victory over death.[8]

TIME TRANSFORMED

So the resurrection of Jesus Christ in time has utterly transformed the way we look at history, at eternity, at the year, at the week, and at every day!

> After the Easter night comes the morning, and then another night and another new day. Time begins again, but it is now filled from "inside" with that unique and truly "eschatological" experience of joy. . . . Time itself is now measured by the rhythm of the end and the beginning, of the end transformed into beginning, of the beginning announcing the fulfillment.[9]

He is alive! He is risen indeed!

[*Worship Notes* 2.4, April 2006]

---

8. Schmemann, *For the Life of the* World, 50–51.
9. Schmemann, *For the Life of the* World, 58–59.

3

A Resurrection Concordance

(New Testament references to Christ's resurrection outside of the gospels)

Acts	1 Corinthians	1 Thessalonians
1:3, 22	6:14	1:10
2:24, 31, 32	15:4, 12–17, 20, 21	4:14
3:15, 26		
4:2, 10, 33	2 Corinthians	2 Timothy
5:30	4:14	2:8
10:40, 41	5:15	
13:30, 34, 37		1 Peter
17:3, 18, 32	Galatians	1:3, 21
25:19	1:1	3:18
26:8, 23		
	Ephesians	Revelation
Romans	1:20	1:18
1:4	2:6	
4:24		
6:4, 5, 9	Philippians	
7:4	3:10	
8:11, 34		
10:7, 9	Colossians	
14:9	2:12	
	3:1	

[*Worship Notes* 2.4, April 2006]

4

The Glory of Easter
Others' Reflections

Sometimes I think about how different the world would be had Jesus not resurrected from the dead. Although the disciples would not risk their lives trumpeting a new faith in the streets of Jerusalem, neither would they forget him. They had given three years to Jesus. He may not be the Messiah (not without Easter), but he had impressed them as the wisest teacher ever and had demonstrated powers that no one could explain.

After time, as emotional wounds began to heal, the disciples would seek some way to memorialize Jesus. Perhaps they would collect his sayings in a written form akin to one of our Gospels, though with the more sensational claims excised. Or, along with Jews from that period who were honoring other martyr-prophets, they might build a monument to Jesus' life. If so, we who live in modern times could still visit that monument and learn about the carpenter/philosopher from Nazareth. We could sift through his sayings, taking or leaving whatever we liked. Worldwide, Jesus would be esteemed in the same way Confucius or Socrates is esteemed.

In many respects I would find an unresurrected Jesus easier to accept. Easter makes him dangerous. Because of Easter I have to listen to his extravagant claims and can no longer pick and choose from his sayings. Moreover, Easter means he must be loose out there somewhere. Like the disciples, I never know where Jesus might turn up, how he might speak to me, what he might ask of

THE GLORY OF EASTER

me. As Frederick Buechner says, Easter means "we can never nail him down, not even if the nails we use are real and the thing we nail him to is a cross."

Easter puts Jesus' life in a whole new light. Apart from Easter I would think it a tragedy that Jesus died young after a few short years of ministry. What a waste for him to leave so soon, having affected so few people in such a small part of the world! Yet, viewing that same life through the lens of Easter, I see that was Jesus' plan all along. He stayed just long enough to gather around him followers who could carry the message to others. Killing Jesus, says Walter Wink, was like trying to destroy a dandelion seed-head by blowing on it.[1]

Tomorrow we shall celebrate the glorious Resurrection of Christ. I shall be remembering you in the Holy Communion. Away with tears and fears and troubles! United in wedlock with the eternal Godhead Itself, our nature ascends into the Heaven of Heaven. So it would be impious to call ourselves "miserable." On the contrary, Man is a creature whom the Angels—were they capable of envy—would envy. Let us lift up our hearts![2]

Christ passed through the wall into the upper room, and yet He was able to eat while there. This is a problem for us because it never occurs to us that He passed through the wall because the wall was ghostly, and not because Christ's resurrection body was.[3]

Apart from the resurrection, Jesus has no more claim upon us than Socrates, Abraham Lincoln, Mohandas Gandhi, Martin Luther King, Jr., or Anwar Sadat: He was simply one among many good leaders who managed to meet an unjust death.[4]

Not Friday, the day of His death, but Sunday, the day of His resurrection, was the Lord's day; and to that day belonged their highest act of worship, when they showed forth His death victoriously in the eucharist, while He Himself, their risen Lord, was present in their midst.[5]

---

1. Yancey, *Jesus I Never Knew*, 225–26.
2. Lewis, "Letter of March 27, 1948," in *Collected Letters*.
3. Wilson, *Credenda Agenda* 14.3, 13.
4. Stookey, *Calendar*, 49.
5. Maxwell, *Outline of Christian Worship*, 4.

PART 9. THE CHURCH YEAR

The resurrection of Jesus Christ is the heart's greatest celebration. It is the highest note in our songs of triumph, and the loudest echo in our shouts of praise. It takes us to the depths of our heart's true joys, and causes our hope to climb to new heights. It brings wings to our faith and courage to our souls. It is victory's banner, and freedom's proclamation. It is the great Yes to all the promises of God. At the manger we celebrate why Jesus came for us, at the cross we celebrate what He did for us, and at the empty tomb we celebrate all that He has for us.[6]

The resurrection was a kind of cosmic explosion that reverberated in all directions. It gave the followers of Jesus a new understanding of the present, but also of the past and of the future. Through the resurrection (and that alone) the cross, that instrument of capital punishment by the hated Romans, ceased to be an enigmatic embarrassment and became the central symbol of the faith.[7]

The eucharist as celebrated in the Church after our Lord had risen from the dead, is not merely, and was never intended to be, a simple re-enactment of the Last Supper. It has been transfigured by the glorious fact of the Resurrection; and the glory of the Lord shines round about it, as in this supreme act of Christian worship men offer to Him an oblation of all possible praise, showing forth His death and victory, rejoicing in His real presence among them, and looking for His coming again to judge the world in righteousness.[8]

O God, who for our redemption gave your only begotten Son to death on the Cross, and by his glorious resurrection has delivered us from the power of our enemy: Grant that we who celebrate with joy the day of our Lord's resurrection, may be raised from the death of sin by your life-giving Spirit. Grant us so to die daily to sin, that we may evermore live with him in the joy of his resurrection, empowered and transformed by your grace in and among us.

O Lord, so stir up in your church, indeed in each of us, that Spirit of adoption and reconciliation that is made possible by your grace revealed in Jesus the Christ, that we being renewed in both body and mind, may worship and serve you in sincerity and truth.

---

6. Lessin, source unknown.
7. Stookey, *Calendar*, 37)
8. Maxwell, *Concerning Worship*, 15–16.

We pray this in the name of the same Jesus Christ our Lord who lives and reigns with you and the Holy Spirit, one God, now and forever. Amen.[9]

[*Worship Notes* 2.4, April 2006]

---

9. *Book of Common Prayer.*

5

The Road to Understanding
An Easter Meditation
(Luke 24:13–35)

INTRODUCTION

How small and distant God can seem when we're discouraged! Two of Jesus' disciples faced that kind of disappointment and discouragement as they wearily made their way from Jerusalem to a village called Emmaus on the Sunday afternoon after their Master had undergone a horrible execution on a Roman cross.

THE WALK

Two disciples—apparently not two of the 12 disciples, but two of the larger group mentioned, for example, in 24:9—had left the gathering of disciples; they had seemingly given up hope and were returning home. They were "unemployed disciples," so to speak; as one writer puts it, they were "walking home from a funeral." As they go, they are discussing the recent events in Jerusalem, and it is clear from the narrative that they are disheartened and discouraged (see 24:14, 18–21).

But then Jesus overtakes them and walks with them. They don't recognize at this point that it is Jesus who is walking with them. Various and sometimes fanciful theories have been advanced for this lack of recognition: he was unrecognizable from the beatings and the crucifixion; he looked so different in his resurrected body (but later they would indeed recognize him); the two were so upset they didn't look up; they were walking west and the sun was in their eyes!

But verse 16 in fact tells us why they didn't recognize Jesus: "their eyes *were prevented* from recognizing him." This is most likely an instance of what is termed in biblical studies a "divine passive"—where a passive verb is used without attribution to show that it is God who is acting. And this certainly seems to be the case here: God is supernaturally keeping them from realizing until later who is speaking to them as they walk down the road to Emmaus.

THE LESSON

In 25–27 we have an account of the greatest Bible lesson ever given! As Jesus relates to the disciples what they should have known and understood about the necessity of Christ's death and glorification from the Old Testament Scriptures. Undoubtedly he covered many areas of prophecy, types, and foreshadowings of his Person and ministry in the sacrificial system and other parts of the Old Testament. What an amazing privilege to hear the Old Testament expounded by the One whom it foretold!

The disciples invite him to stay with them, and then at table prevail upon him to say the blessing, probably in recognition of his status as a teacher, which they had just experienced. And we read: "their eyes *were opened*" (31). Here again is the divine passive: God had prevented their eyes from recognizing Jesus, and now he opens their eyes. He closed their eyes, and now he opens them. And then and only then, when God decides to make it possible, do the disciples recognize him. But Jesus immediately vanishes from their sight. Excitedly they ask each other: "Did not our hearts burn within us while he talked to us on the road, while he opened to us the Scriptures?" (32).

And so the two disciples hurry back to Jerusalem, and there learn that Jesus has appeared to Simon (Peter) also; they tell their story as well (33–35).

PART 9. THE CHURCH YEAR

THE SIGNIFICANCE

Luke is probably writing sometime around A.D. 60, long after the ascension and the ceasing of Jesus' post-resurrection appearances. He is writing to a generation that no longer has the opportunity to physically see the resurrected Christ. His readers are just "ordinary" disciples, not apostles or eyewitnesses: ordinary disciples, like us, who live by faith in a risen Lord whom we have not seen, but which we believe we one day will see in all his glory.

Even though the two disciples do get to see the risen Christ, actually the most significant and lasting thing happens to them *before* they realize who is talking. This may well be why Luke (and the Holy Spirit through Luke) is relating this incident to us.

To see this point, let us consider the obvious structure of the passage; there are two contrasting parts, characterized by contrasting directions, atmospheres, attitudes, and moods. One writer has recognized this fact by entitling the story: "A Solemn One-Way Trip Becomes a Joyous Roundtrip."[1] The two halves look like this:

Part 1

1. the disciples are going from Jerusalem to Emmaus, slowly and sadly
2. Jesus appears
3. their eyes are prevented from recognizing him

Part 2 (the reverse)

3. their eyes are opened and they do recognize him
2. Jesus disappears
1. the disciples rush back from Emmaus to Jerusalem, quickly and joyfully

The centerpiece and pivot of the account is of course the teaching that Jesus gives to the disciples. And it is crucial to see that God does not

---

1. Walther, "A Solemn One-Way Trip."

allow them to recognize Jesus until *after* they have received his Bible lesson concerning himself. Their eyes, having been *closed*, are not *opened* (31) until "he *opened* to us the Scriptures (32); the same Greek word is used for "opened" in both of these verses.

Jesus wants their faith in him and his resurrection to rest upon the Scriptures' witness to himself, not upon a fleeting experience of his risen presence. His gentle upbraiding of them leading up to his lesson revolves around their failure to understand what the prophets had taught in the Old Testament (25); and it was this deficiency that his explanation was intended to address (26). They were discouraged because they were "foolish" and "slow of heart to believe" that what had transpired in the last few days had all been part of God's plan ("it was necessary that the Christ should suffer," 26), and that events had *not* spun out of his control.

This is what Jesus wants them to understand, so that they then might stand firmly on God's Word as a firmer foundation for future faith than an exhilarating, but ephemeral, experience with him. Their experience would then serve to reconfirm the truth of Scripture—not the other way around. They have only a split second of experience with the risen Christ once their eyes were opened and they recognized him—he vanishes immediately. But their hearts are now full of God's predictions and promises concerning his Messiah. They were beginning to understand the need for, and the sense of, Jesus' death and resurrection—and they understood that *from the Scriptures*.

Seeing the risen Christ was an important witness to his victory over death, but more importantly it was an affirmation and confirmation of the truth of God's promises—we see this later at the very end of Luke 24 again: Jesus appears to all the disciples and "*opened* their minds to understand the Scriptures" (45–46; the same Greek verb again). The Scriptures were to serve as the foundation for their faith and their ministry (47–48).

Paul's preaching likewise was founded in the Scriptures. He says in 1 Corinthians 15, "Now I make known to you, brethren, the gospel which I preached to you. . . . For I delivered to you as of first importance what I also received, that Christ died for our sins *according to the Scriptures*, and that he was buried, and that he was raised on the third day *according to the Scriptures*" (3–4). God has provided a sure and steady foundation for faith in the witness of the Scriptures: the Old Testament, and now the New Testament as well.

And this is the significance of the passage for Luke's readers as well. Hardly any of them would have seen Christ in the flesh, before or after the resurrection. Luke was writing in a time when there were no more resurrection appearances. Believers' relationship with Christ could not be built on an experience of seeing him. The significance of Luke's account here is that there is a foundation for faith which is even more important than seeing the risen Christ, and this foundation is still available for believers: the foundation of God's revelation in the Scriptures. As Jesus said to Thomas in John 20:29: "Blessed are those who have not seen and yet have believed." And this faith comes through the Scriptures.

We need to acknowledge the secondary role of experience. Our spiritual experience is important, but must always be informed and guided and channeled by the Word. It's because of the testimony of Scripture that we understand who Christ is and what he has done and how we can join the family of God through faith in him.

The two disciples in this account got to physically see the risen Christ and have all their doubts, fears, and disappointment instantly swept away by the glory of his physical, resurrected presence. But that is not likely to occur in our situation; the normal pattern for ordinary disciples (like you and me) is to build our faith on the witness of the Scriptures—its testimony to God's sovereign control over all things is the cure for discouragement.

LESSON FOR OUR WORSHIP

There is a clear implication for our worship as well. We must strive to "let the word of Christ dwell in you richly" (Col 3:16) by making sure that our worship times are based on, structured around, saturated with, and enriched by the Scriptures (see part 1, chapter 2: "Word-Saturated Worship"). That will ensure a true and deep experience of God in both our private and our corporate worship.

[*Worship Notes* 4.4, May 2009]

ASCENSION

6

The Neglected Ascension

> Popular conversations about the incarnation tend to focus on the nativity stories and on the earthly life of Jesus. . . . Many think that the ascension really means the shedding of Jesus' human nature, as if Jesus is now simply a spiritual presence who used to be human, someone whom we remember with affection rather than someone we expect to see face to face someday. A full-orbed understanding of the incarnation will also proclaim that the incarnation continues, that it is the incarnate Christ who has ascended. Jesus is our contemporary not a historical figure from a dead past. He is living now, interacting with us now, and standing now in a human body in the presence of the Father. He is praying for us now, leading our worship now, feeling our pain now, sharing our humanity now.[1]

Indeed, the ascension of Jesus Christ is too quickly skipped over (or ignored) in many churches. Yet it is an event with enormous implications for our lives and for the life of the church:

1. Jesus has been exalted and has taken his place of rulership at his Father's right hand (1 Tim 3:16; Col 3:1; Eph 1:20–21).

---

1. Smit, "Incarnation Continues," 4.

2. Jesus serves now as our Advocate and Intercessor in the Father's presence (1 John 2:1; Heb 7:25).

3. For the first time, humanity dwells in the Father's presence in heaven, guaranteeing that we will also follow Jesus there one day (John 14:2–3; 1 Cor 15:23).

4. Jesus went and sent the Holy Spirit to dwell in us and with us (John 7:39; 16:7).

5. Christ our Mediator in his continuing humanity and eternal priesthood (1 Tim 2:5; Heb 4:14, 15; 5:6; 6:20; 7:17, 21; 8:1; 10:21) serves the heavenly tabernacle (Heb 8:1–2) and actively leads his people into the Father's presence in worship. (Heb 2:12; 10:19–22).

Christ has indeed returned to the glory which he had with the Father before the world was (John 17:5)—but now with one amazing and crucial difference: in the incarnate Son of God, deity and humanity are inseparably fused forever. And so when Christ returns to the Father and ascends the throne, in himself he takes humanity where it has never been before. There is now a man seated at the right hand of the Father in heaven!

That has enormous import for our future (see #3 above), but also for our present. Alexander Schmemann makes the following interesting observation:

> We must understand that the real tragedy of Christianity is not its "compromise" with the world and progressive "materialism," but on the contrary, its "spiritualization" and transformation into "religion." And religion—as we know already—has thus come to mean a world of pure spirituality, a concentration of attention on matters pertaining to the "soul."[2]

The result, Schmemann points out, is that many Christians see their faith as an escape from the world and tend to divorce their "religious" activities from their everyday lives. But in Christ's incarnation and ascension we see the elevation and sanctification of humanity, renewing in fallen people the glory of being created in the image of God and making all aspects of life holy and an appropriate offering of worship to the Father (Rom 12:1; 1 Cor 10:31). The Man on the throne, the Head and Bridegroom of the Church, does not take his—or our—humanity lightly!

---

2. Schmemann, *For the Life of the World*, 48.

THE NEGLECTED ASCENSION

[*Worship Notes* 2.5, May 2007]

7

An Ascension Concordance

(New Testament references to Christ's ascension and session at the right hand of the Father)

Matt 22:44; 26:64
Mark 12:36; 14:62; 16:19
Luke 22:69; 24:51
John 3:13; 6:62; 14:2–3; 17:1–5, 25; 20:17
Acts 1:9–11, 22; 2:24, 31–34; 3:15, 26; 4:2, 10, 33; 5:30–31; 7:55–56; 10:40, 41; 13:30, 34, 37; 17:3, 18, 32; 25:19; 26:8, 23
Rom 1:4; 4:24; 6:4, 5, 9; 7:4; 8:11, 34; 10:7, 9; 14:9
1 Cor 6:14; 15:4, 12–17, 20, 21, 23, 25
2 Cor 4:14; 5:15
Gal 1:1
Eph 1:20–21; 2:6; 4:8–10
Phil 2:9–11; 3:10
Col 2:12; 3:1–2
1 Thess 1:10; 4:14
1 Tim 3:16
2 Tim 2:8
Heb 1:3, 13; 4:14–16; 7:25; 8:1; 10:12; 12:2
1 John 2:1
1 Pet 1:3, 21; 3:18, 22
Rev 1:18

AN ASCENSION CONCORDANCE

[*Worship Notes* 2.5, May 2007]

8

A Service of Worship for Ascension Sunday

(Second Presbyterian Church, Memphis, Tennessee, May 28, 1995)

(Note the readings on the ascension from many sections of the Bible: Psalms, gospels, epistles, Revelation)

CHORAL INTROIT: "Sing Ye to the Lord."   Titcomb
Sing ye, sing ye to the Lord
Who ascended to the heav'n
To the glory of the Father.
Alleluia! Alleluia!

CALL TO WORSHIP   Luke 24:50–53
When he had led them out to the vicinity of Bethany,
he lifted up his hands and blessed them.
While he was blessing them,
he left them and was taken up into heaven.
Then they worshiped him
and returned to Jerusalem with great joy.
And they stayed continually at the temple, praising God.

A SERVICE OF WORSHIP FOR ASCENSION SUNDAY

HYMN OF ASCENSION: "Hail the Day That Sees Him Rise" LLANFAIR

PRAYER OF ADORATION

READING FROM THE GOSPELS　　　　　　　　John 14:1–6
    This is the Word of God.
        All glory be to God on High
        and to the Lamb upon the throne.

READING FROM THE EPISTLES　　　　　　　　Ephesians 1:15–23
    This is the Word of God.
        All glory be to God on High
        and to the Lamb upon the throne.

READING FROM THE APOCALYPSE　　　　　　Revelation 4:2–4, 9–11
    This is the Word of God.
        All glory be to God on High
        and to the Lamb upon the throne.

RESPONSIVE READING FROM THE PSALMS　　Psalm 47

Liturgist:
    Clap your hands, all you nations;
Choir:
    Shout to God with cries of joy.
Congregation:
    How awesome is the Lord Most High,
    the great King over all the earth!

Liturgist:
    He subdued nations under us,
Choir:
    Peoples under our feet
Congregation:
    He chose our inheritance for us,
    the pride of Jacob, whom he loved.

PART 9. THE CHURCH YEAR

Liturgist:
>God has ascended amid shouts of joy,
>the Lord amid the sounding of trumpets.

Choir:
>Sing praises to God, sing praises.

Congregation:
>**Sing praises to our King, sing praises.**

Liturgist:
>For God is the King of all the earth;
>sing to him a psalm of praise.

Choir:
>God reigns over the nations;

Congregation:
>**God is seated on his holy throne.**

Liturgist:
>The nobles of the nations assemble
>as the people of the God of Abraham,

Choir:
>For the kings of the earth belong to God;

Congregation:
>**He is greatly exalted!**

HYMN OF EXALTATION: "Crown Him with Many Crowns" DIADEMATA

PRESENTATION OF GIFTS TO THE EXALTED CHRIST

OFFERTORY ANTHEM: "Alle, Alleluia!..............Marion Reinhart
Alle, alleluia! Alle, alleluia!
The Son of Man must be deliv'r'd into the hands of sinful men,
And He must be crucified, and on the third day rise again,
And then He will ascend, and be seated on the throne. Amen.

A SERVICE OF WORSHIP FOR ASCENSION SUNDAY

CONGREGATIONAL RESPONSE......... LASST UNS ERFREUEN
A hymn of glory let us sing;
New songs thro'out the world shall ring:
Alleluia! Alleluia!
Christ, by a road before untrod,
Ascendeth to the throne of God.
Alleluia! Alleluia! Alleluia! Alleluia! Alleluia!

PRAYER OF THANKSGIVING AND DEDICATION

GREETINGS

PRAYER FOR ILLUMINATION

READING FROM THE ACTS OF THE APOSTLES Acts 18:1–22

> All men are like grass, and all their glory is like the flowers of the field;
> **The grass withers and the flowers fall,**
> **but the Word of our God stands forever. Amen.**

SERMON

PRAYER OF COMMITMENT

HYMN OF CHRIST'S DOMINION: "Jesus Shall Reign" DUKE STREET

BENEDICTION

CONGREGATIONAL THREEFOLD AMEN

[*Worship Notes* 2.55, May 2007]

9

A Responsive Reading for Ascension Sunday

(First Evangelical Church,
Memphis, Tennessee, May 28, 1995)

Leader: Jesus said to her, "Stop clinging to me, for I have not yet ascended to the Father," but go to my brethren, and say to them, 'I ascend to my Father and your Father, and my God and your God.'"

Cong: **God raised him from the dead, and seated him at his right hand in the heavenly places, far above all rule and authority and power and dominion, and every name that is named, not only in this age, but also in the one to come.**

Leader: If then you have been raised up with Christ, keep seeking the things above, where Christ is, seated at the right hand of God.

Cong: **Set your mind on the things above, not on the things that are on the earth.**

Leader: Who is the one who condemns? Christ Jesus is he who died, yes, rather who was raised, who is at the right hand of God, who also intercedes for us.

A RESPONSIVE READING FOR ASCENSION SUNDAY

Cong: **We have such a high priest, who has taken his seat at the right hand of the throne of the Majesty in the heavens.**

Leader: Since then we have a great high priest who has passed through the heavens, Jesus the Son of God, let us hold fast our confession.

Cong: **For we do not have a high priest who cannot sympathize with our weaknesses, but One who has been tempted in all things as we are, yet without sin.**

All: **Let us therefore draw near with confidence to the throne of grace, that we may receive mercy and may find grace to help in time of need.**

(John 20:17; Eph 1:20–21; Col 3:1–2; Rom 8:34; Heb 4:14–16)

[*Worship Notes* 2.55, May 2007]

PENTECOST

Pentecost is the climax of Eastertide, the "Great Fifty Days," and commemorates when the Holy Spirit fell upon Jesus' followers, as related in Acts 2.

10

The Holy Spirit and Worship

BEAUTIFULLY COMPLEMENTARY ROLES

See part 6, chapter 1 for a consideration of the mutually deferential and harmonizing roles of Father, Son, and Holy Spirit.

CHRIST AND THE SPIRIT

Association

There is a strong association between Christ's ministry and the Holy Spirit. Isaiah says that the Spirit will be "upon" the coming Messiah in a special way (11:1–2; 42:1–2; 61:1). And the Holy Spirit is closely associated with the coming of Jesus into the world: he is said to either be "upon" or to be "filling" Mary (Luke 1:35), Elizabeth (1:41), Zechariah (1:67), Simeon (2:25), and John the Baptist (1:25).[1]

Likewise the Spirit is powerfully active at Christ's conception (Matt 1:18,20; Luke 1:35), baptism (Matt 3:16; John 1:32–34), and temptation (Matt 4:1; Luke 4:1, 14); and in his ministry (Matt 12:15-21, 28; Luke 4:18–19, 10:21), death (Heb 9:14), and resurrection (Rom 1:4; 1 Tim 3:16).[2]

Continuation.

Jesus hints at a continuation of his earthly ministry, after his ascension, through the coming Holy Spirit. He promises the disciples that he (John 15:26) and the Father (14:16) would send another (of the same kind) Paraclete (Comforter/Counselor/Helper, as it is variously translated). The Holy Spirit will bear witness about Christ (John 15:26) and bring to the disciples' remembrance what Jesus said (14:26). As Ferguson puts it:

> The ministry of the Spirit stands in total continuity with that of the Son. Like Jesus, the Paraclete is sent by the Father and comes from the Father. Jesus is the truth, the Paraclete is the Spirit of truth who leads Christians into the truth (John 14:6, 17; 15:26; 16:13); Jesus is the teacher of his disciples (14:23, 26); the Paraclete comes to teach them further. Jesus is the witness God has sent; the Paraclete is sent into the world to be a witness (18:37; 15:26). The world does not know or accept Jesus (5:43; 12:48); nor does the world recognize the Paraclete (14:17). In all of these senses the Paraclete is the one who "takes what belongs to Jesus" (cf. 16:14).[3]

Identification

As a result, the Spirit's ministry is inseparably intertwined with the Person and work of Christ. Paul and Peter even refer to the Holy Spirit as "the Spirit of Christ" (Rom 8:9; 1 Pet 1:11). Ferguson explains that when the Spirit "comes to Christians to indwell them, he comes as the Spirit of Christ in such a way that to possess him is to possess Christ himself, just as to

---

1. Ferguson, *Holy Spirit*, 32–33.
2. Ferguson, *Holy Spirit*, 71–72.
3. Ferguson, *Holy Spirit*, 56.

lack him is to lack Christ. . . . To have the Spirit of Christ is to be indwelt by Christ."[4]

The practical outworking of the Spirit's close identification with Christ is that he is "thus qualified to reshape us to be 'like Christ', from one degree of glory to another (2 Cor 3:17–18). This is the central function of the Holy Spirit in the life of the Christian believer."[5] To which adds Gregory Dix, "'To walk after the Spirit' and for 'Christ to live through me' means for St. Paul the same thing."[6]

Glorification

Amazingly, the Spirit takes on a role of subordination within the Godhead: "He will not speak on his own authority," but rather mediate the Father's and Son's teaching (John 16:13); and he will glorify Christ rather than draw attention to himself (John 16:14). J. I. Packer expresses beautifully the essence of this wonderful truth:

> Think of it this way. It is as if the Spirit stands behind us, throwing light over our shoulder, on Jesus, who stands facing us. The Spirit's message is never, "Look at me; listen to me; come to me; get to know me" but always, "Look at him, and see his glory; listen to him, and hear his word; go to him, and have life; get to know him, and taste his gift of joy and peace." The Spirit, we might say, is the matchmaker, the celestial marriage broker, whose role it is to bring us and Christ together and ensure that we stay together.[7]

"There is no worship directly ascribed to the Holy Spirit anywhere in the New Testament."[8] Yet the Spirit is fully God, and is therefore worthy of worship—"with the Father and the Son together is worshiped and glorified," in the words of the Nicene Creed. So hymns and other expressions of worship which honor him, especially when the entire Trinity is being praised, are certainly appropriate. However, it would seem clear that a church that focuses on the Spirit to such an extent that there is not a primary emphasis on Christ and his work is not truly being led by the Spirit, nor honoring

---

4. Ferguson, *Holy Spirit*, 37, 54.
5. Ferguson, *Holy Spirit*, 56.
6. Dix, *Shape of the Liturgy*, 260.
7. Packer, *Keep in Step with the Spirit*, 66.
8. Wainwright, *Doxology*, 93.

him and his own desires. When a church is lifting up the person and work of Christ, that is a sure sign that the Spirit is at work!

OUR WORSHIP AND THE SPIRIT

The bottom line to all the above is that the Holy Spirit is committed to actualizing our worship in and through Jesus Christ in the body of Christ and in our personal lives.

Enabled by the Spirit

As we have seen, the Holy Spirit's ministry may be seen as an extension of what Christ has done and is doing. The same holds true for worship. "Worship, through the presence and action of the Holy Spirit, is a meeting . . . between Jesus Christ and his people."[9]

In part 5, chapter 2 we looked at Christ's role in leading our worship: in his humanity he is the one Mediator between us and God in our response of worship; he is "in the midst of the congregation," leading us in singing the Father's praise (Heb 2:12). Yet in his humanity he is physically present at the Father's right hand, interceding for us (Heb 7:24) and serving as the minister in the true sanctuary in heaven (8:1–2). So how can he be present among us as well? (He is omnipresent in his deity, of course, but not in his humanity.) Reggie Kidd suggests that "the union between the Son and the Holy Spirit within the Trinity and the functional . . . representation of the Son by the Holy Spirit mean that when the Holy Spirit ministers among us, Christ Himself is present. . . . Christ sings in the church by means of the Holy Spirit . . . and that's why Christ [in his humanity] can "be in two places at once."[10]

Gerrit Dawson explains this mystery thus:

> The glorified, ascended, still incarnate Jesus is in the Holy Place, within the true tabernacle (Heb 8:2) of which every earthly house of worship is at best a shadow. Yet in the Holy Spirit he is not removed from us. The Spirit is the Spirit of Jesus, and brings his presence to us in worship, most especially in the preaching of the Word and the administration of the sacraments. And the Spirit lifts us up, spiritually, in our worship to the throne of God where

9. von Allmen, "Worship and the Holy Spirit," 130.
10. Reggie Kidd, email correspondence.

Jesus serves as our advocate, priest, intercessor and worship leader. Through the Spirit, then, the ascended Jesus comes to be in our midst and through the same Spirit we are brought in Christ our High Priest into the Father's welcoming presence.[11]

So, we might say, Christ is the *way*, and the Holy Spirit is the *guide*.

Motivated by the Spirit

As Christopher Cocksworth puts it, "The new humanity of Christ in which we share by the Spirit, is doxological by nature. He gives glory to the Father in the Spirit. To enter the realm of Christ's humanity is to step into a life of worship."[12] Von Allmen adds, "Worship is the automatic outcome of the outpouring of the Holy Spirit upon the Church."[13] To be in Christ (2 Cor 5:17; 1 Pet 5:14) and to be indwelt by him (John 14:20; 17:22–23) thus means to be a worshiper. And it is the Holy Spirit who baptizes us into Christ and energizes the process of sanctification by which we grow progressively in Christlikeness—becoming, as part of that process, more willing and wholehearted worshipers.

The role of the Spirit in worship is to open our hearts to Christ—to take what we know in our heads and drive it into our hearts; to engender thankfulness and praise for his grace, his love and his presence; and then through and in Christ to draw forth our praises to the Father. "The Son eternally gives glory to the Father in the Spirit. . . . Christian worship is participation in this . . . life of God through the presence and activity of the Holy Spirit in the life of the believer and in the midst of the fellowship of the Church."[14]

As William Nicholls explains it: "If the objective basis of our worship is the work of Christ, its subjective basis is the work of the Spirit in the individual members of the church, enabling them to hear Christ's Word as God's Word, and to participate personally in His response to the Father."[15] In other words, we *can* come into God's presence in worship because of the (objective) work of Christ (Heb 10:19–22); but we *want to* come into God's presence because of the (subjective) work of the Holy Spirit in our hearts.

11. Dawson, *Jesus Ascended*, 136.
12. Cocksworth, *Holy, Holy, Holy*, 185.
13. von Allmen, "Worship and the Holy Spirit," 130.
14. Cocksworth, *Holy, Holy, Holy*, 189–90.
15. Nicholls, *Jacob's Ladder: The Meaning of Worship*, 58.

The Spirit completes in us the biblical cycle of Revelation and Response (part 2, chapter 1)), taking the revelation of God and driving it home to our hearts, thus drawing forth our response of worship.

Empowered by the Spirit

The true power of New Covenant worship rests not in our own efforts to lift up to God an appropriate and worthy response of praise; but rather in the continuing mediating ministry of Christ, who offers to the Father as our representative and High Priest a perfect response of praise (part 5, chapter 2). And the Holy Spirit empowers our worship thus as he connects us to that perfect offering: by identifying us with Christ (Rom 8:9–11); by assuring us that we are children of God (Rom 8:14–17) and brothers of Christ (Heb 2:11); by encouraging us to therefore come boldly into the Father's presence (Heb 10:19–22); and by filling us that we might sing to, praise, and thank the Father through Christ from our hearts (Eph 5:18–20).

The Spirit also empowers our worship by giving gifts to promote the growth, unity and love of the body (Eph 4:1–16). Ferguson states:

> The correlation between the ascension of Christ and the descent of the Spirit signals that the gift and gifts of the Spirit serve as the external manifestation of the triumph and enthronement of Christ [cf. Eph 4:7–8] . . . . Gifts of the Spirit are given to equip the people of God and to enable them to set on display the glory of God, the fullness of Christ, in the temple of God (Eph 4:12, 16).[16]

Here again we see the Christ-centeredness of all the Spirit's doings, even in his most distinctive (and debated) contributions.

As controversial as this whole subject is in the church today (far beyond the scope of this article!), let us remember two defining and limiting qualifications which Ferguson points out: (1) the primacy of God's revealed Word in the ordering and exercise of spiritual gifts (revelation always logically and theologically precedes response); and (2) the goal of love (the "more excellent way" of 1 Cor 12:31 and chapter 13).[17] The Spirit's gifts, as all his works, will always seek to glorify Christ and bring honor to the Father.

[*Worship Notes* 1.9, September 2006]

16. Ferguson, *Holy Spirit*, 207–8.
17. Ferguson, *Holy Spirit*, 208–9.

11

The Spirit's Coming
Some Rich Quotes

> When the Spirit of truth comes, he will guide you into all the truth, for he will not speak on his own authority, but whatever he hears he will speak, and he will declare to you the things that are to come. He will glorify me, for he will take what is mine and declare it to you. (John 16:13-14)

> When the day of Pentecost arrived, they were all together in one place. And suddenly there came from heaven a sound like a mighty rushing wind, and it filled the entire house where they were sitting. And divided tongues as of fire appeared to them and rested on each one of them. And they were all filled with the Holy Spirit and began to speak in other tongues as the Spirit gave them utterance. (Acts 2:1-4)

> The need for a theology about the Day of Pentecost is seen by reflecting on how readily Christians misunderstand the nature of the church. For many people the church is a voluntary organization of individuals and exists primarily for reasons that relate to efficiency.... Because such a gathering is purely voluntary, people feel free to participate when they wish (particularly when they "need" to "get something out of it"), and to do otherwise the rest of the time.
>
> A proper theology of the Day of Pentecost says a resounding "No!" to such popular ideas. The church is a community called

together by the Spirit of the Risen One. It is not something we choose to do (and equally well could choose not to do), but something to which we are summoned. The Greek word for church (*ekklēsia* from which we derive "ecclesiastical") means "those who have been called forth or summoned," much as one is summoned to appear in a court of law. And we are called as a body of interdependent parts, not as separable individuals. The free-spirited individualism of our age is a manifestation of Babel, not Pentecost, as should be evident from the intransigent divisions and intractable conflicts such individualism fosters. The Risen One, who is present at all times and in all places, seeks to bind together by the action of the Spirit all things that have been wrongly separated. Participation therefore is not something we do on the basis of personal choice or need; participation in the Body of Christ is inherent in being Christian. The church, not the individual, is the irreducible unit of Christianity. Further, the church is to be a sign of the future: No matter how haltingly and imperfectly, the church seeks to enact in the present world the justice and grace that characterize the eternal reign of God. Therefore Christians participate in the church not so much for what they can get as for what they can give, for what they can offer as an alternative to the dominant ways of the world. (Laurence Hill Stookey, *Calendar: Christ's Time for the Church*, 76–77)

Pentecost is sometimes spoken of as the "reversal" of Babel, a return to one language. In fact, the crowds heard the disciples in their own tongues (Acts 2:6). There is no suppression of cultural diversity; quite the opposite. The coming of the Spirit means particularity is preserved and indeed encouraged, as Paul's vision of the Spirit-directed Church makes clear (1 Cor 12). (Jeremy Begbie, "Christ and the Cultures: Christianity and the Arts," in Gunton, *The Cambridge Companion to Christian Doctrine*, 116)

He receives that Spirit from the Father for us vicariously in His humanity that out of His fullness He might baptise the Church by the Spirit at Pentecost into a life of shared communion, mission and service. (James F. Torrance, "The Doctrine of the Trinity in Our Contemporary Situation," in British Council of Churches, *The Forgotten Trinity*, 11)

Breathe in me, O Holy Spirit, that my thoughts may all be holy.
Act in me, O Holy Spirit, that my work, too, may be holy.
Draw my heart, O Holy Spirit, that I love but what is holy.

Strengthen me, O Holy Spirit, to defend all that is holy.
Guard me, then, O Holy Spirit, that I always may be holy. Amen.
(attributed to St. Augustine)

The Spirit makes known the personal presence in and with the Christian and the church of the risen, reigning Saviour, the Jesus of history, who is the Christ of faith. Scripture shows . . . that since the Pentecost of Acts 2 this, essentially, is what the Spirit is doing all the time as he empowers, enables, purges, and leads generation after generation of sinners to face the reality of God. And he does it in order that Christ may be known, loved, trusted, honored and praised, which is the Spirit's aim and purpose throughout as it is the aim and purpose of God the Father, too. This is what, in the last analysis, the Spirit's new covenant ministry is all about. . . . The distinctive, constant, basic ministry of the Holy Spirit under the new covenant is so to mediate Christ's presence to believers—that is, to give them the knowledge of his presence with them as their Saviour, Lord, and God—that three things keep happening.

First, *personal fellowship with Jesus* . . . becomes a reality of experience, even though Jesus is now not here on earth in bodily form, but is enthroned in heaven's glory.

Second, *personal transformation of character into Jesus' likeness* starts to take place as, looking to Jesus, their model, for strength, believers worship and adore him and learn to lay out and, indeed, lay down their lives for him and for others.

Third, *the Spirit-given certainty of being loved, redeemed, and adopted* through Christ into the Father's family, so as to be "heirs of God and fellow heirs with Christ" (Romans 8:17), makes gratitude, delight, hope, and confidence—in a word, assurance—blossom in believers' hearts.

By these phenomena of experience, Spirit-given knowledge of Christ's presence . . . shows itself. (J. I. Packer, *Keep in Step with the Spirit*, 47, 49)

During Jesus' lifetime, He ate and drank frequently with the Twelve. He fed 5000 people on one occasion, and 4000 on another occasion. He had other meals and feasts throughout His ministry. But the sum total of people who ate and drank with Jesus during His lifetime would be somewhere in the thousands.

Now He has gone away, and the Spirit has come. Now Jesus is absent in the flesh, but present in the Spirit. And today, in Idaho alone, many thousands are eating and drinking with Jesus. Throughout the world, today, there are millions eating and drinking with Jesus, drawn from every tribe and tongue and nation. Jesus never did that. That could only be done when Jesus went away to His Father, and sent the Helper to be with us. (Blog post by Peter J. Leithart)

[*Worship Notes* 1.9, September 2006]

REFORMATION SUNDAY

12

The Reformation of Worship

October 31 is celebrated in Lutheran parts of Europe, and in Lutheran churches elsewhere, as Reformation Day (or the Sunday before it as Reformation Sunday). This looks back to October 31, 1517, the day on which Martin Luther posted his "95 Theses" onto the church door at Wittenberg, touching off what we now refer to as the Protestant Reformation.

But Reformation Day is a truly a Christian holiday for *all* Protestants, one which deserves to be remembered and celebrated; for it indeed is in many ways our spiritual "Independence Day," as it commemorates the movement of God which freed the church from the medieval distortions of the gospel and restored the apostolic teaching concerning the nature of salvation.

While the crucial reformation and restoration of New Testament doctrine was at the center of the Reformation, there were at the same time important changes in worship that likewise corrected some of the excesses and errors of medieval practice. (As major as the changes were, later movements would go even further in restructuring the forms of worship, such as the Anabaptists.) Geoffrey Wainwright writes:

> The Protestant Reformers sought a root-and-branch cleansing of medieval western doctrine and its liturgical expression. They

returned to the scriptures and, to a lesser extent, the patristic Church, in order to recover the original gospel for both teaching and worship. In the liturgy, they operated both at the level of ceremony, where the pruning was severe, and at the level of the ritual structures and texts, where they set about a drastic reshaping and reformulation.[1]

Some of the most important new, or renewed, worship emphases were:

THE SOLE PRIESTHOOD OF CHRIST

This crucial doctrinal recovery has of course enormous implications for our understanding and practice of worship. (See part 5, chapters 2 and 3.) Thomas Torrance explains:

> At the Reformation this doctrine [justification through Christ alone] had immediate effect in the overthrow of Roman sacerdotalism—Jesus Christ is our sole Priest. He is the one and only Man who can mediate between us and God, so that we approach God solely through the mediation of the Humanity of Jesus, through his incarnate Priesthood. When the Humanity of Christ is depreciated or whenever it is obscured by the sheer majesty of his Deity then the need for some other human mediation creeps in—hence in the Dark and Middle Ages arose the need for a human priesthood to mediate between sinful humanity and the exalted Christ, the majestic Judge and King. There was of course no denial of the Deity of Christ by the Reformers—on the contrary they restored the purity of faith in Christ as God through overthrowing the accretions that compromised it; but they also restored the place occupied in the New Testament and the Early Church by the Humanity of Christ, as he who took our human nature in order to be our Priest, as he who takes our side and is our Advocate before the judgment of God, and who once and for all has wrought out atonement for us in his sacrifice on the Cross, and therefore as he who eternally stands in for us as our heavenly Mediator and High-Priest.[2]

---

1. Wainright, *Doxology*, 263.
2. Thomas Torrance, *Theology in Reconstruction*, 166–67.

THE PRIMACY OF THE WORD AND THE IMPORTANCE OF PREACHING

In the Middle Ages "the sermon had fallen into a grave decline, most parish priests being too illiterate to preach; and the place of the Scripture lections had been usurped on a great many days by passages from the lives and legends of the saints. The Scriptures were not fully accessible in the vernacular.... Reformation was an urgent necessity."[3]

In the Reformation, "helped by the vernacular language, the printed book and the long sermon, worship became ... the vehicle for direct doctrinal instruction of the people."[4]

SCRIPTURE AND WORSHIP IN THE LANGUAGE OF THE PEOPLE

> At the close of the Middle Ages worship in the West was virtually the preserve of clergy and monks. The Daily Offices had been collected together into a single book called the Breviary; another book, the Missal, contained the Mass. Both were in Latin—an academic tongue since the fall of the Roman Empire. This, together with the decline of preaching, resulted in the virtual disappearance of edification from the worship of ordinary people.[5]

The Reformers championed (aided by the recent invention of the printing press) the translation and publication of the Bible in the language of the people; and they insisted on conducting of services in the vernacular, so that the people could fully understand and enter into worship, and be instructed from the Word.

PARTICIPATORY WORSHIP

By the end of the Middle Ages "the great central rite of Christendom had become a drama performed by the clergy in an unknown tongue, a spectacle to be witnessed, but no longer a corporate act of worship."[6]

---

3. Maxwell, *Outline of Christian Worship*, 72.
4. Wainwright, "Periods of Liturgical History," in Jones et al., *Study of Liturgy*, 37.
5. Abba, *Principles of Christian Worship*, 22–23.
6. Abba, *Principles of Christian Worship*, 23.

> [The Reformers] accomplished the formidable task of wrenching worship from the hands of the priests and returning it to the people. This, undoubtedly, was one of the crowning achievements of the Reformation.[7]

CONGREGATIONAL SINGING

What had become the domain of choirs and monks was restored to the corporate expression of the people. Corporate singing became a centerpiece of Protestant worship. Luther himself composed new hymns (in the vernacular) for the people's song, and Calvin instituted the singing of paraphrased Psalms.

REGULAR, MEANINGFUL, AND PARTICIPATORY COMMUNION

> At the beginning of the sixteenth century, the celebration of the Lord's Supper in the Western Church had become a dramatic spectacle, culminating not in communion but in the miracle of transubstantiation, and marked by adoration, not unmixed with superstition, at the elevation. Said inaudibly in an unknown tongue, and surrounded with ornate ceremonial and, if a sung mass, with elaborate musical accompaniment, the rite presented only meager opportunity for popular participation. The people were not encouraged to communicate more often than once a year.[8]

For all their debates about the exact nature of what happened during the celebration of the Lord's Supper, the Reformers were united in their desire to restore Communion to the people as a rich spiritual feast. In Geneva Calvin did not succeed in instituting weekly Communion as he wished, but most traditions coming out of the Reformation provide for at least quarterly, and usually monthly, celebration of the Lord's Supper (and some indeed weekly).

[*Worship Notes* 5.8. October 2010]

   7. Fromm, "New Song."
   8. Maxwell, *Outline of Christian Worship*, 72.

13

Celebrating the "Solas" of the Reformation in Worship

A powerful corporate way to commemorate and integrate the significance of the Reformation for both doctrine and worship is to together proclaim and respond to the distinctive teachings of that movement—often referred to as the "Solas" of the Reformation, based on their Latin designations.

The following litany of readings and song responses has been adapted from a brochure originally published by Beeson Divinity School (and used by permission).

(Congregation) **The Protestant Reformation of the sixteenth century was a tremendous movement of spiritual and ecclesiastical renewal which called the church back to its biblical and evangelical roots. As heirs of this great tradition, we own afresh the principles for which our forebears in the faith struggled, and by which they lived and died.**

    SOLA SCRIPTURA (the Scriptures Alone)
(Leader) The Holy Scriptures have once and for all revealed to us the nature and purposes of God, the work of Christ, the call of the gospel, and the way of salvation.
(Cong.) **You have been born again, not of perishable seed but of imperishable, through the living and abiding word of God; for "All flesh is like**

grass and all its glory like the flower of grass. The grass withers, and the flower falls, but the word of the Lord remains forever." [1 Pet 1:23–25]

> Song of Response:
> How firm a foundation, ye saints of the Lord,
> Is laid for your faith in his excellent Word!
> What more can he say than to you he has said,
> To you who unto Jesus for refuge have fled?

SOLUS CHRISTUS (through Christ Alone)
(Leader) Salvation has been accomplished and is applied solely on the basis of the substitutionary death of Jesus Christ on the cross for our sins.
(Cong.) **Jesus said to him, "I am the Way, the Truth and the Life. No one comes to the Father except through me." ... And there is salvation in no one else, for there is no other name under heaven given among men by which we must be saved."** [John 14:6; Acts 4:12]

> Song of Response:
> **My hope is built on nothing less
> Than Jesus' blood and righteousness.
> I dare not trust the sweetest frame,
> But wholly lean on Jesus' Name.
>> On Christ the Solid Rock I stand,
>> All other ground is sinking sand;
>> All other ground is sinking sand.**

SOLA GRATIA (by Grace Alone)
(Leader) As those who were dead in our trespasses and sins, we could do nothing to earn or deserve God's mercy. Salvation is a free gift of God's grace—his unmerited favor freely bestowed through Jesus Christ and his atoning death.
(Cong.) **For all have sinned and fall short of the glory of God, being justified as a gift by his grace through the redemption which is in Christ Jesus.** [Romans 3:23–24]

PART 9. THE CHURCH YEAR

Song of Response:
> Marvelous grace of our loving Lord;
> Grace that exceeds our sin and our guilt.
> Yonder on Calvary's mount outpoured,
> There where the blood of the Lamb was spilt.
>> Grace, grace, God's grace,
>> Grace that will pardon and cleanse within;
>> Grace, grace, God's grace,
>> Grace that is greater than all our sin.

SOLA FIDE (by Faith Alone)
(Leader) We respond to God's gracious initiative in salvation through personal trust in the Redeemer. Not by our works, but rather by faith in Christ's provision on our behalf, do we enter into the blessings of eternal life.
(Cong.) **Nevertheless knowing that a man is not justified by the works of the Law but through faith in Christ Jesus, even we have believed in Christ Jesus, that we may be justified by faith in Christ, and not by the works of the law; since by the works of the Law shall no flesh be justified.** [Gal 2:16]

Song of Response:
> My faith has found a resting place, not in device nor creed;
> I trust the Everliving One, his wounds for me shall plead.
>> I need no other argument, I need no other plea,
>> It is enough that Jesus died, and that he died for me.
>
> Enough for me that Jesus saves, this ends my fear and doubt;
> A sinful soul I come to him, he'll never cast me out.
>> I need no other argument, I need no other plea,
>> It is enough that Jesus died, and that he died for me.

SOLI DEO GLORIA (Glory to God Alone)
(Leader) God has created and redeemed us in order to display the glory of his majesty and his mercy, the wonders of his greatness and his grace.
(Cong.) **Now to Him who is able to do far more abundantly than all that ask or think, according to the power at work within us, to him be glory in the church and in Christ Jesus throughout all generations, forever and ever. Amen.** [Eph 3:20–21]

Song of Response:
> To God be the glory, great things he has done;
> So loved he the world that he gave us his Son,
> Who yielded his life an atonement for sin,
> And opened the lifegate that all may go in.
>> Praise the Lord, praise the Lord,
>> Let the earth hear his voice!
>> Praise the Lord, praise the Lord,
>> Let the people rejoice!
>> O come to the Father through Jesus the Son,
>> And give him the glory, great things he hath done!

[*Worship Notes* 5.8. October 2010]

CHRISTMAS

14

Worship the King
A Second Look at Matthew 2

> Now after Jesus was born in Bethlehem of Judea in the days of Herod the king, behold, wise men from the east came to Jerusalem, saying, "Where is he who has been born king of the Jews? For we saw his star when it rose and have come to *worship* him."
>
> Then Herod summoned the wise men secretly and ascertained from them what time the star had appeared. And he sent them to Bethlehem, saying, "Go and search diligently for the child, and when you have found him, bring me word, that I too may come and *worship* him."
>
> And going into the house they saw the child with Mary his mother, and they fell down and *worshiped* him. (Matt 2:1–2; 7–8; 11)

PROSKUNÉO

Not to get overly technical (or to ruin anyone's Christmas!), but it is important to recognize an important principle of translation: that is, that there is not necessarily a strict one-to-one correspondence between a word in one language and a single word in another language. That is certainly the case when the Greek Testament is translated into English: scholars talk about a "field of meaning" that a particular Greek word often carries, with different shades of meaning when used in different contexts, hence allowing for (if not necessitating) different translations of that word in different passages.

That seems to be the case in Matthew 2 with the translation of the Greek word *proskunéo*, which in many translations (such as the ESV above, and the King James Version) is translated "worship."

The literal root meaning of *proskunéo* is «to kiss toward,» and from there the term developed the sense «to fall down or prostrate oneself» (as in kissing the ground), and hence ultimately «to worship, adore.» According to David Peterson, the various uses of the term in the New Testament within its field of meaning include:

1. *prostration in homage to royalty* (this is where Peterson puts the use in Matthew 2)

   "Where is he who has been born king of the Jews? For we saw his star when it rose and have come to *worship* Him." (Matt 2:2; also Matt 2:8, 11; 15:19 [mocking])

2. *prostration in homage and entreaty*

   And behold, a leper came to him and *knelt before* him, saying, "Lord, if you will, you can make me clean." (Matt 8:2; also Matt 9:18; 15:25; 18:26; 20:20; Mark 5:6)

3. *institutional worship*

   Now among those who went up to *worship* at the feast were some Greeks. (John 12:20; also John 4:20, 22; Acts 8:27; 24:11; Rev 11:1)

4. *false worship* (of man, angels, Satan)

   Again, the devil took him to a very high mountain and showed him all the kingdoms of the world and their glory. And he said to him, "All these I will give you, if you will fall down and *worship* me." (Matt 4:8–9; also Luke 4:7; Acts 7:43; 10:25; Rev 9:20; 13:4, 8, 12, 15; 14:9, 11; 16:2; 10:10, 20; 20:4; 22:8)

5. *true worship* (inward reverence, with or without outward prostration)

> And behold, Jesus met them and said, "Greetings!" And they came up and took hold of his feet and worshiped him. (Matt 28:9)

> "But the hour is coming, and is now here, when the true *worshipers* will *worship* the Father in spirit and truth, for the Father is seeking such people to *worship* him." (John 4:23; also Matt 4:10; 14:33; 28:9, 17; Luke 4:8; 24:52; John 4:21, 23, 24; 9:38; 1 Cor 14:25; Heb 1:6; 11:21; Rev 4:10; 5:14; 7:11; 11:16; 14:7; 15:4; 19:4, 10; 22:9)[1]

MATTHEW 2

There is no indication that the Magi (or Herod) recognized Jesus' deity; rather it is clearly stated that they were coming to pay honor to a "king." While Matthew certainly has the perspective of Christ's deity, it seems to be reading back to consider worship being in view in this context. "Pay homage" is in fact the rendering in the Phillips translation, the New Revised Standard Version, and the New English Bible.

Don Carson makes the same observation:

> "Worship" . . . need not imply that the Magi recognized Jesus' divinity; it may simply mean "do homage." Their own statement suggests homage paid royalty rather than the worship of Deity. But Matthew, having already told of the virginal conception, doubtless expected his readers to discern something more—viz., that the Magi worshiped better than they knew.[2]

Thus Carson suggests that Matthew, in relating his account in the Greek language to readers with a fuller picture of Christ and his divine nature, knowingly uses a term that in its field of meaning communicates a richer truth than even the original speakers realized. The Magi may have consciously only intended "homage"; but Matthew recognizes and implies that the One who received the homage is indeed deserving of "worship."

David Peterson agrees:

> Although some English versions view this action as "worship" (AV, RSV, NIV), the statement of the Magi in verse 2 suggests that the meaning is homage paid to royalty rather than the worship of deity (so Phillips, NEB; cf. 1 Sam 25:23; 2 Kings 4:36). Of course, Matthew's opening chapter has pointed to Jesus' divine sonship,

---

1. Peterson, *Engaging with God*, 85.
2. Carson, *Matthew*, 86.

and the evangelist no doubt intended his readers to discern that this homage had a greater significance than the visitors from the East could have imagined. Their attitude to Jesus anticipated the submission of the nations to the risen Lord, which is the essence of discipleship according to Matthew 28:16–20. The immediate context in Matthew 2, however, does not demand that worship of Jesus as Son of God is yet in view.[3]

Another effect of reserving the translation of "worship" for a clearer contextual warrant would be to highlight the profoundly significant fact that the first use of *proskunéo* in the New Testament with the clear meaning of worship would then be found in Matthew 4:9–10. There the Second Adam's declaration, "You shall worship the Lord your God, and him only shall you serve," reverses the first Adam's refusal to "glorify God as God" (Rom 1:21; cf. 1:22–25), giving a new trajectory to human history.

In summary: Jesus is worthy of it all! Let us pay homage to him as King, bow before him as Lord, worship him as God!

[*Worship Notes* 6.12, December 2011]

---

[3]. Peterson, *Engaging with God*, 84–85.

15

A Christmas Festival of Lessons and Carols

Since 1989 our church, along with many other churches, has presented a *Festival of Lessons and Carols* as the climax and highlight of our Christmas worship celebrations.[1] You can read about the history of the event at King's College, Cambridge in the U.K. at tinyurl.com/landcarols. The practice has been adopted and tweaked by many different traditions; for one example see tinyurl.com/landcarols2.

THE STRENGTHS OF A LESSONS AND CAROLS SERVICE

Its structure

The structure of the service itself perfectly reflects the Revelation/Response paradigm of all true worship: God first speaks to us through his Word, and we respond with our hymns, songs, carols and prayers. (See part 2, chapter 1.)

---

1. Programs and YouTube video links for a number of these services can be found at worship-resources.org/christmas/.

A CHRISTMAS FESTIVAL OF LESSONS AND CAROLS

Its catechetical nature

The readings and responsive musical numbers walk us through the history of salvation in a vivid, memorable way, progressing from the fall of man through Old Testament's promised redemption to the advent of Christ.

Its participatory nature

The structure allows for the inclusion of a wide representation of the congregation as readers, singers, and players (and also as congregational singers).

Its message

The entire service preaches the gospel the message: a message of wonder, joy, and hope.

Its beauty and power

It is a service of *worship*, not just a concert. The Word of God and its message is central, and allows for the worship response of the people after each lesson. The beloved music of Christmas is enjoyed in the context of the proclamation of the Scriptures, which gives the music added wonder and impact.

THE ELEMENTS OF A LESSONS AND CAROLS SERVICE

The lessons (readings)

The standard readings

The traditional service (used at King's College Cambridge and elsewhere) follows a standard set of readings:

- First Lesson from Genesis 3: 8–15; 17–19. God tells sinful Adam that he has lost the life of Paradise and that his seed will bruise the serpent's head.
- Second Lesson from Genesis 22: 15–18. God promises to faithful Abraham that in his seed shall all the nations of the earth be blessed.

- Third Lesson from Isaiah 9:2, 6–7. The prophet foretells the coming of the Savior.
- Fourth Lesson from Isaiah 11:1–3a, 4a, 6–9. The peace that Christ will bring is foreshown.
- Fifth Lesson from the Gospel of Luke 1:26–35, 38. The angel Gabriel salutes the Blessed Virgin Mary.
- Sixth Lesson from Luke 2:1, 3–7. St Luke tells of the birth of Jesus.
- Seventh Lesson from Luke 2:8–16. The shepherds go to the manger.
- Eighth Lesson from the Gospel of Matthew 2:1–12. The wise men are led by the star to Jesus.
- Ninth Lesson from the Gospel of John 1:1–14. St. John unfolds the great mystery of the Incarnation.[2]

Other possible Scriptures

While these are all powerful readings, there is no inherent need to limit oneself to only these. Our church will vary the readings somewhat (though many of the above still have a regular place, such as the account of the fall in Genesis 3 and the birth narrative in Luke 2), pulling in some other relevant passages:

- Psalm 24:7–10 ("the King of glory")
- Isaiah 7:14 (the virgin birth, Emmanuel)
- Isaiah 11:1–3a (the Branch)
- Isaiah 40:9 ("Behold your God!")
- Isaiah 60:1–3 ("Arise, shine, for your Light has come")
- Micah 5:2, 4–5a (Bethlehem; "He shall be their peace")
- Matthew 2:12, 9b–11a (the Magi)
- 2 Corinthians 8:9; 9:15 ("though he was rich, yet for your sake he became poor")
- Galatians 4:4 ("in the fullness of time")
- Titus 2:11; 3:5 ("the grace of God has appeared")

2. https://anglicancompass.com/nine-lessons-and-carols-a-rookie-anglican-guide/.

A CHRISTMAS FESTIVAL OF LESSONS AND CAROLS

- Hebrews 1:1–6 or 1:5–8; or 1–3a followed by 1:3b–6 (the superiority of the Son)
- Hebrews 2:14–17 or 2:9, 14–15 (he became flesh to die for us)
- Hebrews 12:1–2 ("looking to Jesus")
- 1 Peter 1:8–9 ("though you have not seen him, you love him")
- 1 John 3:1a; 4:9–11 (the love of God for us)

Other sources for readings

Obviously the lessons are Scripture lessons, but we have even used for one of the later readings this selection from *The Valley of Vision*:

> O Source of all good,
> What shall I render to you for the gift of gifts,
> your own dear Son?
>
> *Herein is wonder of wonders:*
> He came below to raise me above,
> was born like me that I might become like Him.
>
> *Herein is love;*
> when I cannot rise to Him He draws near on wings of grace,
> to raise me to Himself.
>
> *Herein is power;*
> when Deity and humanity were infinitely apart,
> He united them in indissoluble unity,
> the uncreated and the created.
>
> *Herein is wisdom;*
> when I was undone, with no will to return to Him,
> and no intellect to devise recovery,
> He came, God-incarnate, to save me to the uttermost,
> as Man to die my death,
> to shed satisfying blood on my behalf,
> to work out a perfect righteousness for me![3]

And once we even included a powerful passage from a Christmas sermon by Spurgeon.

---

3. "Gift of Gifts," in Bennett, *Valley of Vision*.

The theme

Obviously the theme is the birth of Christ! But often we have looked at the Christmas story from varying angles, with an overarching sub-theme giving direction and focus to the individual lessons and to the homily. Here are some examples from services we have done in the past:

We Beheld His Glory (2012)

>His Glory Foreshadowed (Gen 3:8–15)
>His Glory Foretold (Isa 7:14; 9:6)
>His Glory Foreseen (Isa 60:1–3)
>His Glory Incarnated (Luke 2:1–7)
>His Glory Heralded (Luke 2:8–12)
>His Glory Celebrated (Luke 2:13–14)
>His Glory Witnessed (Luke 2:15–20)
>His Glory Adored (Matt 2:1–2, 9b–11a)
>His Glory Veiled (2 Cor 8:9; 9:15)
>His Glory Revealed (John 1:10–14)
>His Glory Eternal (Heb 1:1–6)

The Dawn of Redeeming Grace (2013)

>The Darkness (Gen 3:8–15)
>The Promise of the Light (Isa 11:1–3a)
>The Anticipation of the Light (Isa 60:1; 9:2,6)
>The Bearer of the Light (Luke 1:39–41a, 46–50)
>The Advent of the Light (Luke 2:1–7)
>The Celebration of the Light (Luke 2:13–14)
>The Wonder of the Light (Luke 2:15–20)
>The Homage to the Light (Matt 2:1–2, 10–11)
>The Glory and Grace of the Light (John 1:14–16)
>The Light of the World (Heb 1:5, 7–8, 6)

Lost in Wonder, Love and Praise (2014)

>The Wonder of Promise (Gen 3:8–15)
>The Wonder of Incarnation (Isa 7:14)

The Wonder of Hope (Isa 9:2, 6–7)
The Wonder of His Birth (Luke 2:1–7)
The Wonder of the Shepherds (Luke 2:8–12)
The Wonder of the Angelic Throng (Luke 2:13–14)
The Wonder of Divine Humility (Luke 2:15–20)
The Wonder of the Divine Gift (1 John 1:14, 11–13)
The Wonder of Divine Love (1 John 3:1; John 3:16)
The Wonder of Divine Sacrifice (1 John 4:9–10)
The Wonder of His Future Reign (Heb 1:5–8)

Gift of Gifts (2016)

The Gift of Mercy (Gen 3:8–15)
The Gift of Promise (Isa 7:14; 9:6–7)
The Gift of Hope (Isa 11:1–3a)
The Gift of Service (Luke 1:26–27; 30–35, 38)
The Gift of Joy (Luke 2:1–7)
The Gift of Good News (Luke 2:8–12)
The Gift of Glory (Luke 2:13–14)
The Gift of Peace (Luke 2:15–20)
The Gift of Worship (John 1:1–4, 14)
The Gift of Life (Heb 2:14–17)
The Gift of Gifts (Heb 1:1–4, 6)

The readers

Many churches use just a single reader for all the lessons, often the pastor. But we have found that a Lessons & Carols service gives the opportunity to involve a number of people from the congregation besides just the musical ones. So we use a different reader for each lesson.

For the past several years, in the first of our two identical morning services, we have used readers each of whom was born in another country. This is one way to honor the diversity in our midst and to proclaim that Christ came into the world to save people from every tribe, tongue, and nation. One year we had each read the lesson in his or her native language; but that proved to be hard for most of the congregation to follow and really enter in. So now they all read in English; yet the array of different accents still gives the service a beautiful sense of diversity. (Each year also during the second service we host an International Brunch; internationals are invited to attend the first service, then attend this low-key outreach event during the second.)

In the second service we then use readers spanning all the age groups in the church, from children through senior adults. (We don't have enough internationals to staff a second service of readers anyway.) This too is a unifying approach, and gives a group of men, women, youth, and children an active role to play in worship which they might otherwise never have. Usually we have the youngest reader read the birth story itself, Luke 2:1–7 (making sure he or she is coached ahead of time on how to pronounce "Quirinius"!).

The carols

Response to each lesson

The "carols" (be they for congregation, choir, soloist, or whatever) will normally correspond thematically with the reading with which it is paired. In this way, there is an immediate musical response to the truth expressed in each lesson.

Diversity of style

One of the beauties of a Lessons and Carols service (unlike most prepackaged Christmas "cantatas") is that the segmented structure lends itself to the juxtaposition of a rich variety of styles of music: classical to contemporary, Celtic to Creole, plainsong to gospel. The diversity can be quite invigorating, being expressive of some of the many ways the birth of Christ can be and has been celebrated in song.

It is an opportunity to work in some global songs as well. There are plenty of Christmas resources from other countries available. One year our choir presented a medley of carols from seven different countries, each in its own original language! (Russian, German, French, Spanish, Polish, etc.) Learning the transliterated texts was pretty challenging (and evinced not a few good-natured grumbles from the choir!), but it ended up being an effective and enjoyable endeavor.

The original Festival calls for the Processional to always be "Once in Royal David's City" (with a child or adult soprano singing the first verse a cappella); but there is no reason why this first slot cannot be filled with any number of festive opening anthems.

Variety of forces

The structure of the service also allows for a variety of different musical forces as well: choir, soloists, ensembles, children's choir, men and ladies of the choir, orchestral numbers. Allowance should definitely be made for as much congregational participation as possible: people of course love to sing the traditional carols of Christmas; and they can also take part in carol medleys, as well as some familiar contemporary Christmas songs.

One year we had two ballet dancers do a tasteful and beautiful interpretive dance to the choir's "Climb to the Top of the Highest Mountain." It is my experience that you can get away with some things in a special Christmas service that might not go over so well any other time of the year!!

The homily

Our pastor will take five to ten minutes, close to the end of the service, to bring to a focus our theme and to present the gospel in a gentle and winsome way. In a sense the entire service is the message, and the pastor draws the application and invites a response.

Normally the homily will be followed with one or two more musical numbers, often preceded by one last Scripture lesson. We end with a big celebrative carol with the congregation taking part; a few times we have concluded with the "Hallelujah Chorus," with the congregation singing along on that too.

CONCLUSION

Of course the wondrous happenings of the Christmas story, and its profound implications for the world, never grow old. The Festival of Lessons and Carols format is a rich way to celebrate the old, old story in ever new and fresh ways.

[*Worship Notes* 12.6, June 2017; 12.7, July 2017]

Bibliography

Abba, Raymond. *Principles of Christian Worship*. New York: Oxford University Press, 1966.
Alexander, Eric. "Worship: The Old Testament Pattern" (taped message). Philadelphia: Philadelphia Conference on Reformed Theology, 1998.
Allen, Ronald, and Gordon Borror. *Worship: Rediscovering the Missing Jewel*. Reprint edition. Eugene, OR: Wipf and Stock, 2000.
Allmen, Jean-Jacques von. "Worship and the Holy Spirit." *Studia Liturgica* 2, no. 2 (1963) 124–35.
———. *Worship: Its Theology and Practice*. London: Lutterworth, 1968.
Anderson, Bernhard W. *Out of the Depths: The Psalms Speak for Us Today*. Philadelphia: Westminster, 1974.
Anderson, Ray S., ed. *Theological Foundations for Ministry: Selected Readings for a Theology of the Church in Ministry*. Grand Rapids: Eerdmans, 1979.
Bailey, Kenneth E. *The Good Shepherd: A Thousand-Year Journey from Psalm 23 to the New Testament*. Downers Grove, IL: InterVarsity, 2014.
Barker, Ken, ed. *Songs for Praise and Worship*. Nashville: Word Music, 1992.
Bartholomew, Craig G., et al. *Canon and Biblical Interpretation*. Scripture and Hermeneutics Series, vol 7. Grand Rapids: Zondervan, 2015.
Basden, Paul, ed. *Six Views on Exploring the Worship Spectrum*. Counterpoints. Grand Rapids: Zondervan, 2004.
Bavinck, Herman. *Reformed Dogmatics, Volume 2: God and Creation*. Grand Rapids: Baker, 2004.
Bennett, Arthur, ed. *The Valley of Vision: A Collection of Puritan Prayers and Devotions*. Edinburgh: Banner of Truth Trust, 1975.
British Council of Churches. *The Forgotten Trinity: Selection of Papers Presented to the BCC Study Commission on Trinitarian Doctrine Today*. London: Churches Together in Britain, 1992.
Brueggemann, Walter. *The Psalms and the Life of Faith*. Minneapolis: Fortress, 1995.
Butin, Philip. *Revelation, Redemption, and Response: Calvin's Trinitarian Understanding of the Divine-Human Relationship*. New York: Oxford University Press, 1995.
Calvin, John. *Commentaries on the Epistle to the Hebrews*. Translated by John Owen. Grand Rapids: Eerdmans, 1949.
———. *Institutes of the Christian Religion*. Edited by John T McNeill. Louisville: Presbyterian, 1960.

BIBLIOGRAPHY

Carson, D. A. *Commentary on Matthew*. The Expositor's Bible Commentary, Volume 8. Grand Rapids: Zondervan, 1984.

———, ed. *Worship by the Book*, Grand Rapids: Zondervan, 2002.

Chapell, Bryan. *Christ-Centered Worship: Letting the Gospel Shape Our Practice*. Grand Rapids: Baker Academic, 2009.

———. "Profile of Today's Evangelical Church." Audio message (source unknown).

Cocksworth, Christopher. *Holy, Holy, Holy: Worshipping the Trinitarian God*. London: Darton, Longman and Todd, 2004.

Craigie, Peter. *Psalms 1–50*. Word Biblical Commentary, second ed. Grand Rapids: Zondervan, 2016.

Cranfield, C. E. B. "Divine and Human Action: The Biblical Concept of Worship." *Interpretation* 12, no. 4 (October 1958) 387–98.

Cummings, Brian, ed. *The Book of Common Prayer: The Texts of 1549, 1559, and 1662*. Oxford; New York: Oxford University Press, 2011.

Dawn, Marva. *Reaching out without Dumbing down: A Theology of Worship for the Turn-of-the-Century Culture*. Grand Rapids: Eerdmans, 1995.

Dawson, Gerrit Scott. *Jesus Ascended: The Meaning of Christ's Continuing Incarnation*. Presbyterian & Reformed, 2004.

Dix, Dom Gregory. *The Shape of the Liturgy*. New ed. New York: Continuum, 2005.

Due, Noel. *Created for Worship: From Genesis to Revelation to You*. Fearn, Scotland: Mentor, 2005.

Fee, Gordon D. *God's Empowering Presence: The Holy Spirit in the Letters of Paul*. Grand Rapids: Baker Academic, 2011.

Ferguson, Sinclair B. *The Holy Spirit*. Contours of Christian Theology. Downers Grove, IL: InterVarsity, 1996.

Fettke, Tom. *The Celebration Hymnal: Worship Resource Edition*. Nashville: Word Music, 1997.

Fromm, Chuck. "New Song: The Sound of Spiritual Awakening (A Study of Music in Revival)." Paper presented to Oxford Reading & Research Conference, July 1983.

Fry, Steve. "Unity, Worship, and the Presence of God." *Discipleship Journal*, December 2002.

Furr, Gary, and Milburn Price. *The Dialogue of Worship: Creating Space for Revelation and Response*. Faithgrowth. Macon, GA: Smyth & Helwys, 1998.

Gaddy, C. Welton. *The Gift of Worship*. Nashville: Broadman, 1992.

Goldingay, John. *Psalms*. Baker Commentary on the Old Testament. Grand Rapids: Baker Academic, 2006.

Gunton, Colin S. *The Cambridge Companion to Christian Doctrine*. Cambridge Companions to Religion. Cambridge: Cambridge University Press, 1997.

Hooker, Morna Dorothy. "Adam in Romans 1." *New Testament Studies* 6 (1959–60) 297–306.

———."A Further Note on Romans 1." *New Testament Studies* 13 (1966–67) 181–83.

Horton, Michael. *Pilgrim Theology: Core Doctrines for Christian Disciples*. Grand Rapids: Zondervan, 2013.

Hustad, Don. *True Worship: Reclaiming the Wonder and Majesty*. Wheaton, IL: Hope, 1998.

Jones, Cheslyn, et al. *The Study of Liturgy*. New York: Oxford University Press, 1978.

Kauflin, Bob. *Worship Matters: Leading Others to Encounter the Greatness of God*. Wheaton, IL.: Crossway, 2008.

Keathley, J. Hampton. "Names of God." https://bible.org/series/names-god

Kidd, Reggie. *With One Voice: Discovering Christ's Song in Our Worship*. Grand Rapids: Baker, 2005.

BIBLIOGRAPHY

Kidner, Derek. *Genesis*. Kidner Classic Commentaries. Downers Grove, IL: IVP Academic, 2019.

———. *Psalms 1–72: An Introduction and Commentary on Books I and II of the Psalms*. The Tyndale Old Testament Commentaries. London: InterVarsity, 1973.

Leithart, Peter. *From Silence to Song: The Davidic Liturgical Revolution*. Moscow, Idaho: Canon, 2003.

Lewis, C. S. *Collected Letters, Volume 2: Books, Broadcasts, and the War, 1931–1949*. New York: HarperCollins, 2004.

———. "On Church Music." In *Christian Reflections*. Reissue ed. Eerdmans, 2014.

———. *Reflections on the Psalms*. San Francisco: HarperCollins, 2017.

Luther, Martin. *What Luther Says: A Practical in-Home Anthology for the Active Christian*. Edited by Ewald M. Plass. Saint Louis, MO: Concordia, 2006.

MacArthur, John. *The Ultimate Priority*. Chicago, IL: Moody, 2012.

Man, Ron. *Dallas Seminary Worship Preparation for Future Pastors* (D.Min. dissertation). Dallas: Dallas Theological Seminary, 2007.

———. "False and True Worship in Romans 1." *Bibliotheca Sacra*, no. 157 (March 2000) 26–34. (Also at https://worship-resources.org/2023/06/08/false-and-true-worship-in-romans-118-25/.)

———. *Let Us Draw Near; Biblical Foundations of Worship*. Eugene, OR: Cascade, 2023.

———. "A Letter from Tapescrew (with apologies to C. S. Lewis." *Reformed Worship* 93 (September 2009). https://www.reformedworship.org/article/september-2009/letter-tapescrew. (Also at https://worship-resources.org/2023/06/09/a-letter-from-tapescrew-with-apologies-to-c-s-lewis/.)

———. "More from Tapescrew." *Reformed Worship* 97 (September 2010). https://www.reformedworship.org/article/september-2010/more-tapescrew. (Also at https://worship-resources.org/2023/06/09/more-from-tapescrew/)

———. *Proclamation and Praise: Hebrews 2:12 and the Christology of Worship*. Eugene, OR: Wipf and Stock, 2007.

———. "Tapescrew Letter 3." https://worship-resources.org/2023/06/09/tapescrew-letter-3/.

———. "Tapescrew Letter 4." https://worship-resources.org/2023/06/09/tapescrew-letter-4/.

Martin, Ralph P. *The Worship of God: Some Theological, Pastoral, and Practical Reflections*. Grand Rapids: Eerdmans, 1982.

Maxwell, William D. *Concderning Worship*. London: Oxford University press, 1949.

———. *An Outline of Christian Worship: Its Development and Forms*. London: Oxford University Press, 1936.

Moule, C. F. D. *Worship in the New Testament*. Bramcote, Nottingham: Grove, 1989.

Nicholls, Charles Geoffrey William. *Jacob's Ladder: The Meaning of Worship* Louisville: John Knox, 1955.

Newbigin, Leslie. *The Open Secret: An Introduction to the Theology of Mission*. Grand Rapids: Eerdmans, 1995.

Packer, J. I. *Keep in Step with the Spirit: Finding Fullness in Our Walk with God*. Revised and enlarged ed. Grand Rapids: Baker, 2005.

Paquier, David. *Dynamics of Worship: Foundations and Uses of Liturgy*. Philadelphia: Fortress, 1967.

Peterson, David. *Engaging with God: A Biblical Theology of Worship*. Downers Grove, IL: InterVarsity, 2002.

Pinson, J. Matthew, ed. *Perspectives on Christian Worship: 5 Views*. Perspectives. Nashville: B&H Academic, 2009.

Piper, John. "Our High Priest Is The Son of God Perfect Forever." Sermon preached at Bethlehem Baptist Church, Minneapolis, December 8, 1996. https://www.desiringgod.org/messages/our-high-priest-is-the-son-of-god-perfect-forever.

———. "Preaching as Worship: Meditations on Expository Exultation." https://christianleaders.org/mod/page/view.php?id=32439.

———. "Worship God! (Revelation 22:8–9)." Sermon preached at Bethlehem Baptist Church, Minneapolis, November 9, 1997. https://www.desiringgod.org/messages/worship-god—2.

———. "Worship Is an End in Itself." Sermon preached at Bethlehem Baptist Church, Minneapolis, September 13, 1981. https://www.desiringgod.org/messages/worship-is-an-end-in-itself.

Plantinga, Cornelius, and Sue A. Rozeboom, eds. *Discerning the Spirits: A Guide to Thinking about Christian Worship Today*. Calvin Institute of Christian Worship Liturgical Studies Series. Grand Rapids: Eerdmans, 2003.

Redding, Graham. *Prayer and the Priesthood of Christ*. London: T & T Clark, 2003.

Schmemann, Alexander. *For the Life of the World*. Classics Series, Volume 1. Yonkers, New York: St. Vladimir's Seminary Press, 2018.

Schweizer, Eduard. "Worship in the New Testament." *Reformed and Presbyterian World* 24, no. 5 (March 1957) 197–205.

Segler, Franklin M. *Christian Worship: Its Theology and Practice*. Nashville: Broadman, 1967.

Smit, Laura. "The Incarnation Continues." *Reformed Worship*, March 2006. https://www.reformedworship.org/article/march-2006/incarnation-continues-recovering-importance-ascension.

Smith, Gordon T. *A Holy Meal: The Lord's Supper in the Life of the Church*. Grand Rapids: Baker Academic, 2005.

Sorge, Bob. *Exploring Worship: A Practical Guide to Praise and Worship*. 3rd ed. Grandview, MO: Oasis, 2018.

Spinks, Bryan D., ed. *The Place of Christ in Liturgical Prayer: Trinity, Christology, and Liturgical Theology*. Collegeville, MN: Liturgical, 2008.

Sproul, R. C. *Grace Unknown: The Heart of Reformed Theology*. Grand Rapids: Baker, 1997.

Stookey, Laurence H., *Calendar: Christ's Time for the Church*. Nashville: Abingdon, 1996.

Stott, John R. W. *Romans: God's Good News for the World*. The Bible Speaks Today Series. Downers Grove, IL: InterVarsity, 1994.

———. "Worship" (sermon based on Romans 11:33–36). https://tinyurl.com/stottworship

Torrance, James B. *Worship, Community & the Triune God of Grace*. Downers Grove, IL: InterVarsity, 1996.

Torrance, Thomas F. "The Mind of Christ in Worship: The Problem of Apollinarianism in the Liturgy." In *Theology in Reconciliation: Essays towards Evangelical and Catholic Unity in East and West*. American ed. Grand Rapids: Eerdmans, 1975.

———. "The Word of God and the Response of Man." In *God and Rationality*. Oxford Scholarly Classics Series. New York: Oxford University Press, 2000.

———. *Theology in Reconstruction*. Reprint ed. Eugene, OR: Wipf and Stock, 1996.

Tozer, A. W. *Worship: The Missing Jewel*. Camp Hill, PA: Christian, 1992.

Wainwright, Geoffrey. *Doxology: The Praise of God in Worship, Doctrine and Life; a Systematic Theology*. New York: Oxford University Press, 1984.

———. "The Praise of God in the Theological Reflection of the Church." *Interpretation* 39, no. 1 (1985) 34–45.

Walther, O. Kenneth. "A Solemn One Way Trip Becomes A Joyous Roundtrip!" *Ashland Theological Journal* 14 (1981) 60-67.

Webber, Robert, ed. *The Complete Library of Christian Worship*. 3:120–22). Nashville: Star Song, 1996.

White, James, F. "Making Our Worship More Biblical." *Perkins Journal*, no. 34 (Fall 1980) 38–40.

Willimon, William. *Worship as Pastoral Care*. Nashville: Abingdon, 1990.

Witvliet, John D. *The Biblical Psalms in Christian Worship: A Brief Introduction and Guide to Resources*. The Calvin Institute of Christian Worship Liturgical Studies Series. Grand Rapids: Eerdmans, 2007.

———. "The Trinitarian DNA of Christian Worship: Perennial Themes in Recent Theological Literature." *Colloquium Journal (Institute of Sacred Music, Yale University)*, Autumn 2005. https://ism.yale.edu/sites/default/files/files/The%20Trinitarian%20DNA%20of%20Christian%20Worship.pdf.

———. *Worship Seeking Understanding: Windows into Christian Practice*. Grand Rapids: Baker Academic, 2003.

Wright, N. T. "Freedom and Framework, Spirit and Truth: Recovering Biblical Worship." http://www.ntwrightpage.com.

Yancey, Philip. *The Jesus I Never Knew: Revealing What 2,000 Years of History Have Covered Up*. Grand Rapids: Zondervan, 1997.

Index

Genesis
2:15	32
3:5	69
3:8–19	219
3:16	76
4:26	38, 42
8:18–20	33
12:1–3	76
12:8	38, 42
13:4	38
14:18–20	83–84
14:18–19	39
17:1–2	39
22:15–18	76, 219
26:25	38, 42

Exodus
3	7
3:12	36
3:13–14	36
6:6	36
6:7	37
7:16	33
8:1	33
9:1	33
9:13	33
9:16	40
10:3	33
19:5	37
19:6	34
20:2–3	8
20:4–5	37
20:7	40
33:19	40
34:6–7	36, 37, 38

Leviticus
11:44	40
16	61, 89

Numbers
14:18	38

Deuteronomy
5:10	38
10:21	53
18:18	76
32:3	42

Ruth
1:8	38

1 Samuel
7:12–13	76
12:22	41
16:7	3
25:23	216

INDEX

2 Samuel
7:13	41
7:22	141
9:3	38

1 Kings
3:6	38
18:24	43

2 Kings
4:36	216

1 Chronicles
16:2	43
16:4–5	46
16:7–36	34
16:8	42

2 Chronicles
30:18–20	4

Ezra
9:9	38

Job
1:21	42

Psalms
1:2	12
2:4	53
15:1–2	123
16:11	10
18:1–3	47
20:7	42
22	46
22:1	52, 98–99
22:3	51–54
22:12	52
22:22	11, 99
23	46, 47
23:6	38
24:7–10	220
27:4	46
27:10–12	47
27:10	47
28:9	47
29:2	141
32	46
32:10	38
34:3	10, 11
40:6–8	35
42:1–2	46
47	44, 191
48	44
48:10	11, 12
50:2	46
50:14	35
50:33	35
51	44, 46
51:16–17	35
55:19	53
56:4	11
63:1	46
63:3	38
65:4	46
68:5	47
74:1	47
78:52	47
78:71–72	47
79:13	11, 47
80:1	47, 53
84:1–2	46
84:3	46
84:10–12	46
88	44, 45
89:26	47
95	26
95:1–2	24
95:6	128
95:7	47
96	26
96:4–8	24
96:4	12, 50
96:8	141
98:4	11
99:1–3	53
99:1	53
100	12, 24, 26
100:2	128
100:3–4	11

INDEX

100:3	47	42:8	39, 41
103:13	47	43:6–7	9
105:1	42	43:21	59
107:32	11	48:11	41
110:4	83, 95	52:13–53:12	76
113:2–3	43	57:15	53
114:1–2	33	60:1–3	220
116:4	43	61:1	196
116:13	38	66:2–4	35
116:17	38, 43	66:12–13	47
119:105	121		
123:1	53	**Jeremiah**	
124:8	42	7:21–24	35
131:26	47	9:24	38
135:5	11	17:14	53
135:13	41	31:31–34	35
136	38, 44, 48	32:40	35
138:2	11, 39, 41		
141:2	35	**Ezekiel**	
145:8	38	20:8–9	41
146—150	49	36:22–23	41
148:1–13	10	36:24–28	35
148:5	43		
148:12–13	10, 11	**Hosea**	
149:1	12	6:6	35
150	49, 50		
150:2	12, 36, 125	**Joel**	
		2:32	43

Proverbs

18:19	42

Amos

4:4–6	35

Isaiah

1:10–13	35
6	26
6:2–8	9
7:14	76, 220
9:2	76, 220
9:6–7	76, 220
11:1–9	220
11:1–3	220
11:1–2	196
12:4	43
14:14	19, 69
24:15	43
40:9	220
42:1–2	196

Micah

5:2–5	220
6:6–8	35

Zephaniah

3:9	42

Malachi

1:10	35
1:11	41
1:13–14	35

INDEX

Matthew

1:18	197
1:20	197
2:1–12	220
2:1–11	214–17
2:1–2	220
2:9–11	220
3:16	197
4:1	197
4:8–9	215
4:9–10	217
4:10	58, 216
5:23–24	147
6:1–18	91
6:1–6	65
8:2	215
8:10	66
8:27	66
9:18	215
9:33	66
11:27	99
12:15–21	197
12:28	197
14:33	216
15:19	215
15:25	215
18:26	215
20:20	215
22:35–38	10
22:44	188
23	65
23:23–28	91
23:27–28	65
26:26–28	136
26:27	136
26:64	188
27:46	98–99
27:51	62
28:1	172
28:9	216
28:16–20	217
28:17	216

Mark

3:13	188
5:6	215
12:13	65
12:17	66
12:28–34	65–67
12:30	77
12:33	10
14:22–25	136
14:23	136
15:34	98–99
15:38	62
16:2	172
22:69	188
24:51	188

Luke

1:5–25	10
1:25	197
1:26–55	10
1:26–38	220
1:35	197
1:41	197
1:57–79	10
1:67–79	58
1:67	197
2:1–7	220
2:8–16	220
2:8–14	10
2:25–32	10
2:25	197
4:1	197
4:7	215
4:8	216
4:14	197
4:18–19	197
6:62	188
9:31	58
10:21	197
14:2–3	188
15:1–31	47
22:14–27	136
22:15–18	142
22:16	136
22:17	136
22:18	136
22:19	134, 136
22:42	115
23:39–43	165–66

INDEX

23:45	62
24:1	172
24:13–35	180–84
24:13	172
24:25–27	76
24:36	172
24:45–46	183
24:47–48	183
24:50–53	190
24:52	216

John

1:1–14	220
1:9–11	188
1:18	99
1:22	188
1:32–34	197
2:24	188
4	89–92
4:3–4	90
4:5–9	90
4:10–15	90
4:16–26	91–92
4:20	215
4:21–24	9
4:21	216
4:22	215
4:23–24	121
4:23	77, 92, 216
4:24	216
4:25–26	124
4:27	90
4:32–34	90
4:34	115
5:24	115
5:36–38	115
5:43	197
6:29	115
6:35–58	136
7:16	115
7:39	186
9:38	216
10:17	194
12:20	215
12:48	197
14:1–6	191
14:2–3	186
14:6	91, 197, 211
14:17	197
14:23	197
14:26	197
15:6	124
15:26	197
16:7	186
16:13–14	202
16:13	197
16:14	9, 115, 197, 198
17:1–5	188
17:5	186
17:14–16	142
17:17–18	142
17:25	188
17:26	99
18:37	197
19:30	137
20:1	172
20:17	188
20:26	172

Acts

1:1	99
1:3	175
1:22	175
2:1–4	202
2:16–26	76
2:24	175
2:31–34	188
2:31	175
2:32	175
2:41	160
2:42, 47	160–61
2:46–47	136
3:15	175, 188
3:22–25	76
3:26	175, 188
4:2	175, 199
4:10	175, 188
4:12	211
4:33	175, 188
5:30–31	188
5:30	175
7:2–53	76

INDEX

Acts (continued)

7:43	215
7:55–56	188
8:27	215
9	166
10:25	215
10:40	175, 188
10:41	175, 188
13:30	175, 188
13:34	175, 188
13:37	175, 188
14:15	21
17:3	188
17:18	175, 188
17:32	175, 188
18:1–22	193
20:7	172
24:11	215
25:19	175, 188
26:8	175, 188
26:18	22
26:23	175, 188

Romans

1–11	72
1:2–3	76
1:4	137, 171, 175, 188, 197
1:16–17	76
1:16	22, 165
1:17	167
1:18–32	71
1:18–25	68–70
1:19–20	36
1:20–21	17
1:21–25	217
1:21	19, 20, 32, 57
1:23	20
1:25	19, 20, 32, 57–58, 59
3:9	71
3:18	71
3:21–26	76
3:22	71
3:23–24	211
3:23	71
3:24–25	61, 89
3:24	71
3:25	71
3:26	71
4:5	71
4:24	175, 188
5:1	71
5:2	71
5:11	71
5:12–20	58
5:15	71
5:17	71
5:18	71
5:19	71
5:21	72
6:4	72, 175, 188
6:5	72, 175, 188
6:9	175, 188
6:23	71
7:4	175, 188
8:1–11	72
8:2	137
8:3–4	17, 59
8:4	59
8:9–11	201
8:9	197
8:11	175, 188
8:14–17	17, 201
8:15	72
8:26–27	147
8:26	93
8:34	175, 188, 194
10:7	175, 188
10:9	175, 188
10:14	107
10:17	107
11:30	72
11:33–36	71–74
11:36	17
12–16	72
12:1	17, 59, 77, 186
12:10	17
13:13–14	166
14:9	175, 188
15:5–6	17
15:9	108–9

INDEX

1 Corinthians

1:2	38
1:18	170
1:19	78
5:7–8	76
6:14	175, 188
6:20	137
10:1–4	76
10:14–17	136
10:31	27, 186
11:24–26	136
11:24	136
11:26	136
11:27–34	136
12	203
12:3	v
12:31	201
13	201
14	63
14:24–25	142
14:25	216
15:3–4	183
15:4	188
15:10	94
15:12–17	175, 188
15:20	175, 188
15:21	175, 188
15:23	186, 188
15:25	188
15:45–49	58

2 Corinthians

1:17–19	75–76
1:20	3, 4, 75–78, 86
3:17–18	198
4:14	175
4:18	143
5:15	175, 188
5:17	200
8:9	220
9:15	220

Galatians

1:1	175, 188
2:16	212
2:20	106

3:2	93
3:3	93
3:28	89, 142
4:4	220
5:25	93
6:14	165

Ephesians

1:10	78, 173
1:15–23	191
1:20–21	185, 188, 194
1:20	175
2:1	123
2:6	175, 188
2:13–14	76
2:14–20	89
2:18	86, 108
3:20–21	212
4:1–16	201
4:1–6	7
4:4–6	162
4:8–10	188
4:13–16	143
4:15–16	7
5:18–20	201
5:18–19	7
5:19–21	7
5:19	7
5:26	123

Philippians

1:6	93
2:2–3	10
2:6–8	58, 115
2:9–11	188
2:9	40n
2:12–13	94
3:3	10n, 108, 118
3:4–9	166
3:10	175, 188

Colossians

1:17	v
1:19	77
1:29	94

239

INDEX

Colossians (continued)

2:12	175
3:1–2	194
3:1	175, 185
3:12–17	7
3:12–15	143
3:16	7, 100, 108, 143, 151, 184
3:17	86

1 Thessalonians

1:9	21
1:10	175, 188
4:1	3
4:14	175, 188
5:21–24	94

1 Timothy

1:14–15	166
2:5	98, 107, 186
3:15	185
3:16	188, 197

2 Timothy

2:8	175, 188
3:5	92
3:16–17	121

Titus

2:2–8	17
2:11–12	94
2:11	220
3:5	220

Hebrews

1—2	81–82
1:1–14	81
1:1–2	76
1:2–14	80
1:3	85
1:5–8	221
1:6	98, 101, 216
1:13	188
2:2–3	80
2:6–11	81
2:9–10	85
2:9	82, 98, 221
2:11	98, 103, 201
2:12–18	81
2:12	9, 78, 82, 85, 98–106, 107–8, 117, 142, 152, 186, 100
2:14–17	85, 221
2:14–15	82
2:14	98
2:17	82, 98
2:18	85
3:1	9, 82, 85
3:3	80
3:5–6	76
3:11	85
4:8–9	76
4:14–17	85
4:14–16	81, 188, 195
4:14–15	186
4:15	80
4:16	85, 86
4:18	85
5—10	82–84
5—7	83
5:1	83
5:2	83
5:3	83
5:6	95, 186
5:7–8	85
5:9	83
6:20	186
7:1–16	83
7:2	83
7:5	83
7:7	80
7:11	83
7:15–17	80
7:17–22	76
7:17	95, 186
7:18	83
7:21	80, 95, 186
7:22	80, 83
7:23–25	96
7:24	83, 199
7:25	83, 85, 86, 186, 188

7:26–28	76	10:19–22	8, 22, 62, 84–86, 89, 96, 108, 123, 142, 186, 200
7:26–27	85		
7:26	83	10:19–20	86
7:27	80, 83	10:21	86, 186
7:28	80, 83	10:22	81, 86
8:1–2	8, 84, 85, 186, 199	10:23–25	8
8:1	101, 186, 188	11:6	85
8:2	83	11:21	216
8:4	83	11:39–40	76
8:5	83	12:1–2	221
8:6	80, 81, 83, 85	12:2	86, 188
8:7	83	12:18–24	76, 123
8:10	81	12:18	85
8:11	81	12:22	81, 85
8:19	81	12:24	81, 86
9:7	83	12:28	81, 86
9:8–15	76	13:9–10	76
9:9	83	13:9	81
9:11–14	84, 85	13:10	81
9:11	80, 83	13:11–12	76
9:12	81, 83	13:12	86
9:13	83	13:14	76
9:14–15	81	13:15–16	8
9:14	81, 83, 197	13:15	8, 86, 101
9:15	83	13:20–21	94
9:18–22	83	13:20	86
9:23–24	83	13:21	78, 86
9:23	81, 83, 85		
9:24–26	76	**James**	
9:24	81, 84, 86	1:5	147
9:25–26	83		
9:25	83	**1 Peter**	
9:26	80, 81, 86	1:3	175, 188
9:28	83	1:8–9	221
10:1–18	76	1:10–12	76
10:1	83, 85	1:11	197
10:3	83	1:15–16	95
10:4	83	1:16	40
10:5–9	84	1:21	175, 188
10:10	83, 86, 103	1:23–25	210–11
10:11–14	84	2:4–5	85
10:11	83	2:5	59
10:12–14	86	2:9	59
10:12	81, 83, 188	3:18	175, 188
10:14	81, 83, 103	3:22	188
10:16	81	5:14	200

INDEX

2 Peter
1:12–13 — 4

1 John
2:1 — 186, 188
3:1 — 221
3:2 — 142
4:9–11 — 221

Revelation
1:18 — 175, 188
2:8–9 — 20
4 & 5 — 132
4 — 59
4:2–4 — 191
4:9–11 — 191
4:10 — 216
5 — 59, 60, 142
5:14 — 216
7 — 59
7:11 — 216
9:20 — 215
10:10 — 215
10:20 — 215
11:1 — 215
11:16 — 216
13:4 — 215
13:8 — 215
13:12 — 215
13:15 — 215
14:6–7 — 20, 21
14:7 — 216
14:9 — 215
14:11 — 215
14:16–17 — 60
15:4 — 216
16:2 — 215
19 — 60
19:4 — 216
19:10 — 12, 17, 216
19:20 — 60
20:4 — 215
22:8 — 215
22:9 — 17, 60, 216

www.ingramcontent.com/pod-product-compliance
Lightning Source LLC
Chambersburg PA
CBHW070731160426
43192CB00009B/1394